CONFLICT, PEACE AND HUMAN SECURITY IN SOUTH ASIA

Conflict, Peace and Human Security in South Asia

Edited by

PURNA BAHADUR KARKI

MANOHAR
2026

Reprinted 2026

First published 2025
First eBook edition 2025

ISBN 978-93-6080-321-6 (hardbound)
ISBN 978-93-6080-712-2 (eBook)

Published by

Manohar Publishers & Distributors
4753/23 Ansari Road, Daryaganj
New Delhi 110 002

Cover design by Manoj Kumar

Typeset by Kohli Print, Delhi 110 051

Printed and bound in India

Contents

Tables

Justice

Supreme Court Nepal

Supreme Court
Kathmandu, Nepal

Foreword

In the intricate tapestry of South Asia, the threads of history, politics and human security are interwoven to create a vibrant mosaic. *Conflict, Peace and Human Security in South Asia* is a timely and significant contribution to the understanding of this region's ongoing transformation. This book casts light on pertinent issues with a multifaceted exloration of the challenges and opportunities that lie within the tapestry.

The book opens with an insightful examination of Nepal's political parties, their ideological conviction and democratization of Nepal. It then transitions to the post-conflict political participation of women in Nepal, highlighting the strides made towards gender equality in the political arena—a testament to the resilience and empowerment of Nepalese women.

As we delve deeper, the book addresses the empowerment of crime victims within the Nepali legal framework, reflecting on the nation's journey toward justice and the rule of law. The stability of the democratic constitutions is then scrutinized, underscoring the importance of robust foundations for the sustenance of democracy.

The narrative continues with an analysis of fragmented unions and the social facets of living together in the contemporary societies. It then presents an insight on the Buddhist principles that have shaped the nation's legal and moral compass since mid-nineteenth century. The plight of Bhutanese asylum seekers in Nepal is poignantly portrayed, revealing the cost of the quest for identity and belongings.

China's role in South Asia is critically assessed, considering the economic, geopolitical and cultural implications of its growing influence. This discussion is particularly relevant in the context of the shifting power dynamics within the region and the broader international political landscape.

Each chapter is a window into the soul of Nepal and South Asia, reflecting the region's diversity, its struggles for peace and security and the indomitable spirit of its people. This book is not just a scholarly discourse but a narrative of human experiences, aspirations and the relentless pursuit of harmonious existence.

As we turn pages, we are invited to engage with the ideas and research presented, to question, to reflect and to contribute to the ongoing dialogue about the future of South Asia. I hope that this book will serve as a treatise and a resource for policymakers, academics and everyone interested in South Asia.

I congratulate Dr. Purna Bahadur Karki for his meticulous editorship, and every author for their scholarly contribution.

2 June 2024

DR. MANOJ KUMAR SHARMA
Justice
Supreme Court of Nepal

Justice

Preface

As the editor of *Conflict, Peace and Human Security in South Asia*, I am profoundly honoured to present this timely and significant collection of scholarly works. This edited volume emerges against a backdrop of rapid geopolitical shifts and enduring quests for peace and security within the South Asian region. The chapters herein offer a mosaic of perspectives, each delving into the intricate tapestry of South Asia's political, legal and social landscapes.

The book opens with an incisive analysis of Nepal's political evolution, tracing the rise of communist ideology from the peripheries to the centre stage of mainstream politics. It reflects on the historical and contemporary forces that have shaped the political parties and their ideologies culminating in the establishment of the Federal Republic of Nepal.

In a region where patriarchal norms have long dictated societal structures, the second chapter marks a significant departure by examining the post-conflict political participation of women in Nepal. It is a testament to the resilience and empowerment of women who have emerged from the shadows of conflict to claim their rightful place in the political arena.

The subsequent chapters navigate through the Nepali legal framework, advocating for the empowerment of crime victims and dissecting the foundational elements that contribute to the durability and stability of democratic constitutions. These sections emphasize the importance of robust legal and constitutional frameworks in fostering a just and equitable society.

'Fragmented Unions' offers a critical lens on the social facets of cohabitation within contemporary capitalist societies, while insights from Buddhist principles offer a unique perspective on security issues, reflecting the deep-seated cultural and religious influences that continue to shape South Asian societies.

The plight of Bhutanese asylum seekers in Nepal is poignantly captured in a chapter that explores the tryst with destiny faced by these individuals. The narrative resonates with the broader themes of displacement and statelessness that affect many across the region.

China's expanding role in South Asia is meticulously examined, highlighting the economic, geopolitical and cultural dimensions of its influence. This chapter is particularly relevant in the context of China's growing presence and the implications it holds for the regional power dynamics.

Further, into the intricate dynamics of Nepal-India relations within the broader context of China's growing influence in South Asia this analysis examines Chinese activism in the region and its impact on the United States' long-standing role as a global superpower. It delves into the US foreign and security policy initiatives that shape the peace and stability of Asia, while also considering implications for the US's global superpower status.

Adopting a comprehensive approach, this research scrutinizes the implications of leadership changes in both the US and India, exploring how these shifts affect the power balance in contemporary Asia. It also evaluates policies of the new administration towards US allies, which are pivotal in shaping regional security and stability, heralding a new era in US foreign policy.

Moreover, the study investigates the effects of President Trump's policy of bilateralism, focusing on its long-term positive and negative impacts on US foreign policy in Asia. Finally, it offers insights into the potential benefits of bilateralism for US interests in the economic and security domains.

Each chapter, while distinct in focus, collectively weaves a narrative that is both diverse and interconnected. The authors, through their rigorous research and insightful analyses, invite readers to engage with the complex realities of South Asia—a region that continues to grapple with the dualities of conflict and peace, tradition and modernity and security and vulnerability.

I hope that this book will serve as a valuable resource for scholars, policymakers and anyone interested in the multifaceted issues of conflict, peace and human security in South Asia. May it inspire continued dialogue and contribute to the pursuit of a more peaceful and secure future for all who call this region home.

PURNA BAHADUR KARKI

Acknowledgements

This edited volume is the culmination of efforts and insights from a diverse group of individuals, whose contributions during the article review and selection process have been invaluable. While many of these contributors, hailing from Japan and Nepal, remain unnamed, their support has not gone unnoticed.

I extend my heartfelt gratitude to Senior Lecturer M.M. Ihjas from the University of Peradeniya, Sri Lanka, whose early involvement and guidance have been instrumental to this project. A special thanks goes to my friend Hari Bahadur Khadka of Tribhuvan University, Nepal for engaging in thought-provoking academic debates on contemporary issues. Additionally, the contributions of Aishwarya K.C. and Prakhyat K.C. have been particularly noteworthy.

Above all, my deepest appreciation is reserved for my family—my mother Gaumati Karki, my sisters Sita Kumari K.C. and Rita Kumari Karki, my wife Thapa Kalpana and my children Anmol, Ashima and Aavash. Their unwavering love and support have created a nurturing environment that has been essential to my work. This book would not have been possible without the sanctuary they provide.

1 May 2024 PURNA BAHADUR KARKI

Abbreviations

AMDA	Asian Medical Doctor's Association
BCIM	Bangladesh-China-India-Myanmar
B.P. Koirala	Bishweshwar Prasad Koirala, former Prime Minister of Nepal
BRICS	Brazil, Russia, India, China and South Africa
BRWF	Bhutanese Refugee Women's Forum
BRAVVE	Foundation of Bhutanese Refugee Aiding the Victims of Violence
CA	Constituent Assembly
CBDP	Community-Based Development Programme
CNPC	China National Petroleum Corporation
CPA	Comprehensive Peace Agreement
CPEC	China-Pakistan Economic Corridor
CPN	Communist Party of Nepal
CPN (UML)	Communist Party of Nepal (Unified Marxist-Leninist)
CPN (M)	Communist Party of Nepal (Maoist)
FDI	Foreign Direct Investment
GDP	Gross Domestic Product
GNH	Gross National Happiness
GBV	Gender-Based Violence
GoN	Government of Nepal
HIV	Human Immunodeficiency Virus
IFRC	International Federation of Red Cross and Red Crescent Societies
INGO	International Non-Governmental Organization
KP	Malla Kamal Prakash Malla, a scholar
MLM	Marxism, Leninism and Maoism
MFN	Most Favoured Nation
NATO	North Atlantic Treaty Organization
NC	Nepali Congress

NDA	New Development Bank
OBOR	'One Belt One Road'
OHCHR	The Office of the High Commissioner for Human Rights
PTSD	Post-Traumatic Stress Disorder
SAARC	South Asian Association for Regional Cooperation
SCO	Shanghai Cooperation Organization
SGBV	Sexual and Gender-Based Violence
TCR	Resettlement in a Third Country
TSI	Transitional Solution Initiatives
UCPN (Maoist)	Unified CPN (Maoist)
ULF	United Left Forum
UN	United Nations
UNGA	United Nations General Assembly
UNHCR	United Nations High Commission for Refugees
UNPM	United National People's Movement
USA	United States of America
VT	Vocational Training
WCRWC	Women's Commission for Refugee Women and Children
WFP	World Food Programme
WHO	World Health Organization
WRC	Women's Refugee Commission

CHAPTER 1

Nepal's Political Parties and the Rise of Communists in Mainstream Politics

BHIM NATH REGMI

Nepal—a South Asian country has approximately 26.5 million people occupying a horizontal strip of land between two neighbours India and China. It is an immensely diverse country and the Constitution of Nepal 2015 accepts '. . . Nepal is a multicultural, multilingual, multi-religious, multi-ethnic' by all measures, including geography and caste. Prithvi Narayan Shah appeared ready for battle and determined to bring together the smaller states of Nepal to form a larger nation, is closely linked to the history of modern Nepal. He ruled over all eastern Nepal and a huge part of present Sikkim between that time and his death in 1775. Following him, Rajendra Laxmi and Bahadur established a strong state in the Himalayan region with the support of warriors from Nepal. Nepal is one of the world's most ethnically diverse nations. The issues of castes, classes, or communities in a nation building process become the part of state restructuring. The characteristics of Nepal, never colonized by an external power, are its diverse geography, ethnicity and religion. After killing innocent but brave Nepalese officials in *Kot* and *Bhandarkhal* in 1903 and getting political power from Surendra Bikram Shah, Jung Bahadur Rana initiated a despotic system. He had destroyed all of his main competitors and put his own candidate on the throne and all the key positions and made sure that he was the Prime Minister when it came to making important administrative decisions.[1] King Surendra turned to be a rubber stamp of Rana regime whom the king had granted the power of the King of Lamjung and Kaski districts. For 104 years, Rana rulers practiced all executive powers including the appointment and dismissal of officials and the formulation of Nepalese laws to rule the country and it collapsed in only 1951.[2]

In Nepal, different political events occurred to dethrone Ranas and various political parties were established to institute democratic regime. In 1876, Lakhan Thapa Magar a native from Gorkha district led a systematic political revolt against the Rana rulers and organized local people to revolt against the regime to offer justice to the people. After 55 years of this unsuccessful move, another event of Prachanda Gorkha[3] was established in 1931 to end the Rana regime and help weaken the root of despotic system through public awareness. Praja Parishad[4] was established in 1936 to oust the Rana autocratic rule and the activists of this movement had appealed to the common people to fight for freedom, justice and human dignity. Deepak Thapa and Bandita Sijapati state, 'Nepal Praja Parishad advocated reforms and fermented anti-establishment sentiments among the people. The Rana rulers quickly crushed the movement.'[5] In 1937 the Nepalese Citizen Rights Committee was established to create awareness through pamphlets and articles. The political activists Sukharaj Shastri, Dharma Bhakta Mathema, Dasaratha Chanda and Ganga Lal Shrestha were killed in 1941.[6] Jayatu Sanskritam movement of 1947 was followed by a group of students against the Rana regime. Pramode Shamshere J.B. Rana (1999) states that the protestors called for *Jayatu Sanskritam.*[7] The students of the Tin Dhara Pathshala Sanskrit School in Kathmandu claimed democracy, basic welfare and the insertion of contemporary subjects in their curriculum and it was the first students' political movement (*Gautama,* 2005), which supported the political movement of 1951.[8]

Political parties are imperative to the development of democracy and nation-building. Within the political system, they carry out different tasks. In addition to forming political opinions, they carry out some traditional duties like socialization, recruitment of officials, mobilization and mediation among agencies, the state and society. Political parties are receptive and accountable to society through these actions. As a means of nation-building, they also handle conflicts by providing a forum for social, cultural, political and economic integration. They strive for democracy, justice, equality, inclusion and political empowerment. In practice, political parties play a fundamental role within a well-functioning democracy, representing citizens' interests and verbalizing policies that could support common people's concerns. In the past, especially in developing countries like Nepal, political parties seemed disconnected from the policies to unite people. They pretended to have connected citizens' interests with the political guidelines of the parties. In line with this, the Nepalese political parties, were formed to dismantle the repressive Rana family system and establish a democratic regime in Nepal.[9]

From the above historical perspective, different political movements initiated in Nepalese political history which was essential for setting up a representative democratic system. Hachhethu (2002) views that Nepalese political parties were organized and established 'in opposition to the Rana oligarchy in the country,'[10] and fought for making the people sovereign in history. NC aimed to establish democracy in Nepal—the party leaders were influenced by Indian political movement. Hachhethu (2002) states that the political base of the NC was the same as other political movements and opines, 'Since the parties had emerged with a mission they had suffered from the lack of clarity of thought once their mission to bring an end to the Rana regime was fulfilled through the 1950-1-armed revolution'.[11]

The communist movement officially emerged in Nepal in 1949. Pushpa Lal Shrestha, a member of the NC, had quit the party and joined the communist movement. The party's slogan, at the initial stage, was to fight for 'civil liberties for all the classes' was officially drawn from the guideline of Marxist political theory. The political circumstance of Nepal and structure of Nepali society justified that Nepal was a living reality to heighten the communist movement. Archie Brown (2010) views that Marx secretly thought that people would live more freely than ever under communism and the future society which he predicted as an inevitable stage for human development.[12] Similarly, Hachhethu observes that although the political parties did not initially appear to be ideological groups when they were formed, the CPN adopted the readymade ideologies of Marxism and Leninism with the aim of overthrowing the despotic Rana rule and establishing democracy.[13]

After the end of the Rana regime, Nepalese political parties carried out political democratization and modernization through political education and by articulating public interest. However, in a short time, the political leaders appeared weak to maintain a dynamic leadership for sustaining democracy. Using the constitutional emergency power, King Mahendra seized political power over the State on 15 December 1960, claiming that the NC government, formed in 1959, had failed to uphold law and order, encouraged corruption and prioritized party politics over the interests of the country. The King imposed direct rule, adjourned the constitution, dissolved the elected parliament and the cabinet while imprisoning the then Prime Minister B.P. Koirala as well as his closest allies.[14] The parties were forbidden to organize any activities. After the political coup d'état of 1960, he got a political space to introduce the party-less panchayat system in 1961.[15] As the government was dissolved, Mahendra took over, imprisoning the opponents and establishing an authoritarian regime. He banned political parties outright in favour of a system without the existence of political parties as he believed that they contained antinational elements. In addition, he disapproved of and protested King Tribhuvan's choice to recognize a democratic system and hold an election of constituent assembly.[16] The political leaders, therefore, failed to consolidate the state, 'a state in which the whole is greater than the sum of its parts'.[17] Thereafter, political conflict intensified due to poverty and income inequality. From the beginning, all parties both the NC and the CPN experienced challenges with implementing intraparty democracy and improving the living standard of people. The main leaders chose to nominate the central working committees according to their ways, which ultimately weakened the ideological struggle within the parties. The undemocratic structure of the leading political parties hindered the equal participation of all strata of society further disadvantaging communities that had already been marginalized before the advent of democracy.

The involvement of marginalized groups in politics by the radical communists was a positive sign, garnering significant support from the common people. The poor oppressed politically and socially excluded individuals, along with women benefitted from the open-space programmes of the communists to articulate their aspirations, which helped expand their political programmes. Even the political movements of 1951 and 1990 failed to address the common desire of people. K.P. Malla (1973) argues that the political change of 1951 occurred within a definite political framework and parties had to outline democratic codes to govern the people. After 1951, in the post-democratic era, Nepali intellectuals explored political guidelines, emphasizing that the post-1950 decade was marked by an unprecedented proliferation of intellectual and cultural opportunities, replacing the traditional constraints with a new found liberation and intellect freedom. The decade from 1950 to 1960 is aptly referred to as an extroverted decade, marked by a plethora of ideas, events and coordinated endeavours.[18]

To settle the political issues and achieve the socio-economic progress in the country, the political parties are the main stake holders to implement good policies and set the required plans. However, the parties and the leaders failed to play a significant role which offered the space for political conflicts in different times. The NC holds the title of principal proponent of Nepal's multiparty democracy because of its history of democratic struggle. Despite claiming to support democratic socialism, the NC has historically, supported liberal, centre-right policies. Despite its repeated setbacks by the monarchy in 1960 and 2002, as well as ongoing internal strife, it has played a vital role in Nepal's political evolution establishing a secular and republican government. Although several NC leaders have voiced doubts about federalism and secularism, the party has shown flexibility since the 2006 transition and has, in theory, supported progressive agendas like positive discrimination for marginalized groups and proportional representation.

PARTY CULTURE AND IDEOLOGY

Based on a particular ideological worldview, the leaders mobilize their activists and common people within the party organization and craft new opportunities to rule the country. Every political party made up of a group of people stands unitedly to promote the national interest within a shared set of ideological principles. The agenda of political party celebrates the fact that the party building is for acknowledging its own socio-political goals to maximize intraparty democracy. The ideology of NC endorsed its guideline as 'democratic socialism' from its Birgunj party convention,[19] and aimed to ameliorate for the effective development of the country. The slogan of CPN at its initial convention was 'civil liberties for all classes', with the idea of armed struggle clearly outlined. Some radical communists followed the same doctrine even after 1990, expressing their commitment to the belief that 'Nepal should establish a new democracy as in China, if necessary through armed struggle, so as to create a People's Republic'.[20] For a long time, it remained a firm ideological doctrine of the Maoists and they accepted the principle to transform the country into a socialist state as Lenin had coined in Russia. Similarly, the present Constitution of Nepal (2015) affirms its commitment to socialist democratic norms and values.[21]

Even in 1984, the Royal Palace controlled Nepali politics and the country's central government was disorganized while lacking a clear strategy. The political division between the hard-liner and liberal *panchas*,[22] represented by Lokendra Bahadur Chanda and Surya Bahadur Thapa, deepened as dissatisfaction with the panchayat system grew.[23] If such a political situation develops, the ideology of every political party becomes a governing principle from which the party advances its activities among the people. Ideology and party principles are the central aspects of political parties based on which they train their workers and get the support of the people to achieve their intended political goals. Politically, NC had a strong faith in a liberal economy and since its establishment a huge section of the middle-class people favoured its ideology. In contrast, the CPN brought the voices of the voiceless people, the landless, the oppressed and espoused rural agrarian struggle to fulfil the party mission. Yub Nath Lamsal writes, 'It is the ideology and values that make a political party distinct and different from others.'[24] Nepalese communist parties were established to make the people happier than before, and the first pamphlet of CPN accepted the same feeling. As the principle of Marxism states, 'Karl Marx sincerely believed that under communism—the future society of his imagination which he saw as an inevitable and ultimate, stage of human development—people would live more freely than ever before.'[25]

The political identity of every political party is attached to the political guidelines. The credibility of the party remains among the people for a long, if the party's ideology is shaped by political history, the missions of establishing the party, its objectives and the moral ethics of the leaders. The study of the political culture and ideology of NC and CPN shows that they were established with the same background but look different in their political doctrines. NC adopted democratic socialism whereas CPN's party line embraced the global views of Marxist theory and its doctrine of class struggle. The available sources states that the political parties in Nepal had once again adopted the same political tactic to restore democracy in 1989-90. The coalition movement of Democratic Party NC, United Left Forum (ULF) and United National People's Movement (UNPM)—a group of radical Communists succeeded in restoring democracy in Nepal after 30 years of absolute monarchical rule under the party-less panchayat system. Though NC and the Communist Parties had ideological differences, they united in their goal to liberate the country from an active monarchy. Together, the NC and ULF sought to construct a democratic system in 1990. However, Baburam Bhattarai led the UNPM, which was composed exclusively of ultra-left political groups, including the CPN (Mashal) under Prachanda and the CPN (Mashal) under Mohan Bikram Singh,[26] both of which had adopted a comprehensive democratic agenda. After the formation of the interim government led by Krishna Prasad Bhattarai, the leader of NC in 1990, there was an understanding between NC and leaders of ULF to form a democratic constitution that had issued a directive to the interim government and stated that the King must be a constitutional monarch and act only on the advice of Council of Ministers. Their common agenda was the new constitution must be fully democratic and every law and institution that is in opposition to the democratic values needs to be changed. Every citizen must have access to democratic rights.[27]

Nepal's political parties had an enormous task following the restoration of democracy in 1990 and the democratic movement successfully swapped the active panchayat system which had ruled Nepal for three decades. Restoring multiparty democracy, lifting the prohibition on political parties and curtailing rather than toppling the King's authority were the goals of the 1990 pro-democratic movement. Only with the united action, the political parties could guarantee freedom and equality for all citizens, but it could not happen in practice. It was the main problem of Nepalese political parties that brought a political rift to fuel the grounds for radical communists. For the radical communist parties, the political movement of 1990 could not address the common political reality as it had accepted the political boundary of constitutional monarchy, it automatically widened the gap among the parties. G.P. Koirala, General Secretary of NC, remarked in a mass gathering in Kathmandu, stating that the objectives of the movement were to establish democracy and draft a new constitution, ultimately bringing an end to the constitutional monarchy. Since the King's promises have been broken numerous times throughout history, NC ensured that these demands would be fulfilled this time. The leaders could only accomplish these objectives by remaining united.[28]

Even after the successful political movement of 1990, Nepal faced several hurdles in its ways and people experienced political crises that fuelled the ground for political insurgency. The Constitution of 1991 ignored the voices of common people and the left political parties. Lok Raj Baral (2004) compares the Nepali parliamentary system with the British system and concludes that Nepalese political leaders could not perform well for the people. He notes that the political power struggles of leaders among leaders have led to corruption, fostering an environment where corrupt practices can thrive in the pursuit of power. The likelihood of a stable government and its capacity to carry out policies in an environmentally sound manner have been significantly undermined by the power struggle. Instead of having meaningful and long-lasting policy measures, there have been frequent shifts in the rhetoric surrounding policies from one government to the next.[29] Political party is a part of every modern society and it functions as a group of people organized to achieve constitutional objectives and defend the sovereignty of the people. In a multicultural country like Nepal, political parties play major roles to integrate the citizens and access them to the services of the governing institutions. Samuel P. Huntington observes, 'The function of the party is to organize participation, to bring together separate interests and to serve as the link between social forces and government.'[30]

The CPN (Maoist) adopted the principles of Marxism, Leninism and Maoism as ideological guidelines of the party. After 1990, it regenerated its name from the CPN (Unity Centre) to CPN (Maoism) as its extended Congress decided to adopt 'Marxism-Leninism-Maoism' as the 'ideological direction' of the party. On 22 April 1949, the CPN(CPN) was established and the party accepted 'agrarian revolution as the main policy revolution in Nepal'.[31] Since the beginning, the CPN had adopted to establish 'New People's Republic Political System' guided by the political doctrine of Mao Zedong—and the CPN (Maoist) followed the same guideline when it initiated a decade-long political movement in 1996. The first pamphlet of the CPN in 1949 acknowledged the necessity of launching an armed struggle as the people of Nepal fought for civil liberty through a revolutionary movement. Thus, it should not be restricted to protest using non-violence alone. The anti-people policies of the Rana oligarchy were boycotted by revolutionary committees for civil liberty in every village, town, district, school, college and factory. The party appealed to declare their laws and regulations, organize protests and meetings, seize control of multiple locations to address the demands of labourers, peasants and other workers.[32]

Political parties in every developing country grapple with peripheral political policies and when they do, it can foster consensus among them on major public issues. Social security, economy, health, education, transportation, communication, drinking water and delivery of basic public goods must be the parts of the common agenda for political parties. In Nepal, even after the political movement of 1990, establishing a consensus ruling parties was not a common goal. This lack of unity contributed to the rise in support for the radical communist party, which played a significant role in the political conflict of 1996. In this context, De Sales (2000) argues that the Maoists garnered support largely due to economic grievance, socio-political inequality and injustice.

POST-1990 COMMUNIST PARTIES IN NEPAL

There were many challenges before drafting the constitution in 1991 and a clear rift between left and right-wing political parties was observed. Since the political parties had their political demands they wanted to be incorporated into the Constitution of Nepal which pushed the political parties on different political grounds. Thapa and Sijapati (2006) state '. . . the left was not too happy about a constitution drawn up by a committee and had instated on an election to a constituent assembly, with the radical [political parties] from the UNPM raising up a chorus in support'.[33] The promulgation of the new constitution of Nepal in 1991 had not brought political cheerfulness among the country's different minority groups and radical communist parties which condemned the declaration of the constitution as their demands went politically unfulfilled. Nickson writes the structural problem of Nepalese politics fuelled the ground for radical communists to increase the political support of common people. He states that this process of political polarization is aided by the failure of the parliamentary system to bring about structural reform and the continued decline in the economic status of urban youth and the rural poor, even without any attempt by the monarchy to reclaim its authority. However, if the latter occurred, the message conveyed by *Masal*[34] regarding his disdain for the 1991 Constitution and the parliamentary democracy it established would undoubtedly gain new significance.

These factors suggest that, in contrast to worldwide trends, Nepal's medium-term Maoist prospects are far from exhausted.[35]

The CPN (Maoist) had already begun an open conflict in the rural districts of western Nepal especially in Rolpa and Rukum and according to the party ideology of 'Marxism-Leninism-Maoism', it was keen to implement the path of protracted people's war. At that time, it mobilized the mass and embraced the revolutionary plan for Nepal. It shaped Nepal's strategy and tactics during the People's War in 1995—the party reaffirmed its unwavering commitment to theory of people's war, developed by Mao as universal and unbeatable theory of warfare in China. The commitment was central to their historical initiation of people's war, adopted by the CPN (Maoist) Central Committee in September 1995. This plan is based on the strategy for encircling the urban area from the countryside, tailored to the unique circumstances of our nation. On the other side, the CPN (United Marxist and Leninist) practiced open politics and participated in the government forum. People's multiparty democracy was the NC's political doctrine, and it ultimately agreed to reach a political understanding with the CPN (Maoist) for the peace process. Various political struggles, including those of 1968, the political movement of 1990, and the decade-long movement from 1996 to 2006—especially initiated by the CPN (Maoist) with a forty-point demand presented to the Government of Nepal in 1996—focused on achieving civil liberty through struggle.

The political history of Nepal is marked by various constitutional delays. For the first time, King Mahendra promulgated a new constitution at the beginning of 1959. Then, in 1990, King Birendra accepted constitutional change and it laid the ground for democracy. It accepted the multiparty democracy, with the King serving as Head of State and an executive Prime Minister. It could not endure the political system for a long time and the country experienced a decade long political conflict from 1996. The rise of Communism, even more than the rise of traditional Democratic Party, e.g. NC was the most important political phenomenon of the last decade of the twentieth century and the first decade of the twenty-first century turned out to be a much stronger and long lasting political movement in Nepal as the CPN (Maoist) initiated 'People's War' in 1996. The twelve-point-understanding[36] signed by the seven political parties and the Maoists, which preceded the Comprehensive Peace Agreement (CPA) 2006 pledged to uphold democracy and peace for the advancement of the nation and its citizens. The agreement was signed on 21 November 2006 by the Government of Nepal and CPN (Maoist). An interim constitution was also issued. On 20 September 2015, the new constitution of Nepal came into effect with a resounding majority of votes cast by CA members.[37] Nepal's parliamentary democracy faced Maoist's decade-long political conflict during 1996-2006 and it was followed by the CPA 2006 alarmingly helped increase the supporters of communist groups. Maoist leaders had convinced the people that their demand for CA would offer all sorts of rights to the common people. From the election of the first CA to the present general election, communist parties got the support of rustic as well as urban people. Finally, the country was declared a Federal Democratic Republic, the 240-year-old monarchy was overthrown on 28 May 2008, when the recently elected CA proclaimed Nepal a Federal Democratic Republic.[38] As assumed by the CPN (Maoist) before 1996, their leaders were moving ahead to fight for the people and they believed it would bring real political change in Nepal.

LEAP OF COMMUNISTS IN NEPAL

In the elections to the House of Representatives in 1991 and 1994 more than 33 per cent voters opted for the Communist Party. They received more than 60 per cent of the votes in the post-2008 elections. Even after the political movement of 1951 and general elections of 1958 the socio-economic structure of the country remained same and the feudal group was internally resilient. Due to the political coup by King Mahendra in 1961, the public's perception towards the Communist Party turned positive. In 1963, the NC postponed the political struggle convened by Suvarna Shamser due to national and international political reasons, particularly the 1962 war between Nepal and China which increased the votes of the communists. The communist movement in Jhapa started in 1971[39] and got the support of Nepalese youths. However, due to the national reconciliation policy adopted by the NC in 1976, the policies of the NC became unattractive among the youths. Even the new constitution adopted in 1990 could not change the social and economic structure of Nepalese society, which fuelled the ground for communism in Nepal.[40]

The former CPN (Unity Center), which later became the CPN (Maoist), did not accept the constitution of 1990. The party used the first parliamentary election in 1991, based on the 1990 constitution, to subvert the political system. According to Lenin, new stages of revolution emerge from changes in the power balance at the international level.[41] In 1996, the Maoist struggle took place at the same reality of Lenin's understanding of political revolution. In order to get the people's support for the movement from the stages of the revolution, the United People's Front had submitted forty-point-demand to the government of Nepal in 1996.[42] The leftist political parties in Nepal always focused on the issues of revolution, political guidelines, struggle and transformation of society and connected events like nationality, e.g. the Mahakali Treaty, the killing of the royal family in the palace and the demand of people's rights. Before the 19-day movement in 2006, seven-political-party and the Maoist agreed to hold the round-table conference, announcement of the Interim Constitution and a new constitution drafted and promulgated by the Constituent Assembly got people's verdict in 2008 to receive great support from the Nepalese people.[43] The proclamation of the new constitution by the Constituent Assembly in 2015 and the 2017 elections made Nepal's communists a strong political force, but they failed to use the people's vote.

The history of Nepal's Communist Parties is factionalism.[44] However, they drew the attraction of huge number people in their political organizations and justified that they would be a power centre to change the society.[45] Nepal's peace process was theoretically initiated in 2005 after the signing on the 12-point understanding between the political parties and in Nepalese politics it was a turning point in the history of Nepali politics. Members of civil society, human rights workers and the political leaders of Nepal played a positive role in initiating the dialogue among the parliamentary parties and rebel groups. Even after the initiation of the peace process in Nepal and during the time of both elections of the Constituent Assembly, CPN (Maoist) frequently used it for the new people's movement to bring to a logical end of bringing political achievement in Nepal through the peace process. In a press statement, the leaders announced that the nation now demands that the armed conflict can be resolved amicably and that a lasting peace be established. Therefore, the party is fully committed to ending the autocratic monarchy, holding elections for the Constituent Assembly and ending the current armed conflict through a progressive political outlet with the establishment of a full-fledged democracy to bring about permanent peace.[46]

The political agreement made an understanding to integrate the combatants into Nepalese security forces. It was the victory of Maoists that helped justify their political movement as the previous political movements of Nepal that occurred in 1951 and 1990 failed to address the people's demands. The interesting and unique part of the peace process was the initiation of an open fight between the parliamentary political parties and the Maoists against the monarchical political system of Nepal. After signing the 12-point-agreement, the seven political parties agreed to construct a new political alliance between the seven political parties and the rebel forces that aimed to establish a federal republic country. Ian Martin (2012) acknowledges, 'The 12-point understanding had included the commitment to international supervision of the two armies during the election.'[47] As this, the decade-long political uprising brought some structural changes in legal statutes to mark the socio-economic transformation of Nepal. Earlier, Nepalese intellectuals were the political opponents of Maoists as they had a fear of its political doctrine. Despite that assumption, Maoists were politically admired by many people as they contributed to bringing about many social reforms and changes. In the past, several women, indigenous groups, Madhesi and Dalits were under socio-cultural domination as they felt political marginalization. The Maoists recruited thousands of women in their people's liberation army and it forced the government to recruit women in Nepalese security forces. Baral (2007) considers that Maoist's principle based on Marxist, Leninist and Maoist is redefined to practice in Nepalese context. He further said the Maoists were flexible enough to accept a multi-party system and pluralistic society, which made them compatible to cooperate with the other bourgeois parties. In the first general elections of 1959, CPN had bagged only 4 seats out of 109 whereas Communists got 61.5 per cent votes in the first CA of 2008. After the announcement on new Constitution in 2015, all at once, two largest Communist Parties, i.e. CPN (UML) and CPN (Maoist Center) made a political alliance for the election in 2017 and got 63.27 per cent seats in the Federal Parliament. The decade-long insurgency spawned a political climate that brought about changes in legal statutes, marking socio-economic transformation. In the political arena, it summed up the lived experience of progress for marginal groups from a bottom-up approach, leading to a substantial political shift and the establishment of new power relations. The present Constitution of Nepal endorses a commitment to socialism based on democratic norms and values,[48] reflecting the current ideological and cultural principles of the Nepalese Communist Party.

COMMUNIST PARTIES AT PRESENT

The new post-conflict constitution has fulfilled the expectations of people, which were earlier overlooked in the 1991 constitution. It has set out an overhaul of the political system, devolving significant power from the centre to the seven provinces. People now perceive this as a political tactic of the Maoists, who ultimately succeeded in forming the largest ruling communist party in Nepal. The new party follows the ideological philosophy of Marxism–Leninism, with its political line centred on'People's Democracy'. Their merger to become the Nepal Communist Party has gained political momentum in the country, making it easier to address the people's agenda. Adhikari (2014) states, 'The large proportion of Maoist rank and file belonged to historically marginalized caste and ethnic groups'[49] and with the support of marginal groups, poor people and women, Maoists (Communist) gained popularity in Nepalese politics.

Democracy is always for the happiness of people and every political movement should be for bringing changes in the country. The two remaining communist parties, CPN (UML) and UCPN (Maoist) formed a Left Political Alliance to contest in the recently concluded elections for Nepal's parliament and provincial assemblies. They bagged nearly two-thirds of the seats in the 275-member Federal Parliament and formed governments in six out of seven provincial assemblies. The Left Alliance theoretically was an unexpected coalition between Maoist and Marxist-Leninist parties and now the communist movement in Nepal is facing a crisis as they are not in the same position. The constitutional announcement and the general elections of 2017 politically ended an eleven-year transition from monarchy to federal democracy after a brutal civil war between Maoists and the state. The election is the symbol of the country's socio-political transformation and is an objective of a decade-long conflict. However, the fundamental issue of peace process, i.e. the cases of victims is still unresolved.

After ending the civil war, holding the election of constituent assembly and three levels elections in 2017 and 2022, Nepalese left politics have entered to new phase. Political ideology is shifted to democratic values and norms. The positive development in Nepalese politics has brought sound prospects for strengthening democracy in Nepal. The future course of democratization in Nepal will be measured as a successful tactic if the left political parties uplift the lives of the poor and transform the Nepali economy into a prosperous one. However, the communist parties typically start out with radical and revolutionary rhetoric before gradually transitioning to a social democratic paradigm. Eventually, even the parties that persist in supporting revolutionary socialism will turn into a space for neo-bourgeoisies. The two most powerful moderate communist parties now are UML and Maoist Center, in the realm of legislative politics, these parties are fighting for a position and now they are experiencing an existential dilemma. In Nepali politics, triangle polarization means that there will not be two powerful, moderate communist parties for a very long time. Since one of UML and the Maoist Center will undoubtedly merge. The political coalition between Maoist Center and UML in 2017 was a part of rebirth of communist movement in Nepal and their rift in 2021 was a part of crisis in ideology.

CONCLUSION

Nepalese Communists have achieved significant success in global politics. The promulgation of the Nepalese constitution through CA and inclusion of combatants in security forces legitimized their political agenda of equality, justice, freedom, inclusion and empowerment. By adopting Maoist principles alongside leftist social democratic ideology and transitioning from a decade-long political struggle to the practice of a parliamentary system, they gained widespread popularity at the ballot box. Their experiences from violent war to the peace process, have demonstrated the political struggle of Communists of Nepal in all forms of struggle. This identity of Communists in Nepal remained strong for good reasons. The Maoist Party, an isolated faction of the CPN, was not popular among intellectuals as other political parties of Nepal before 1990. Its regular movement vowed to stand up for the rights of people who were politically voiceless and deprived among others. The Maoist insurgency gradually expanded across the country and finally succeeded in uniting with the next largest communist party is itself a historical move to get the huge support of the Nepalese people. Though, NC had the goal of multiparty democracy, it failed to grasp the support of poor people and stood second in the elections of 2017.

To explore the history of socialism as outlined in the Constitution of Nepal, Nepalese political parties must unite. Now is a time to follow the principles of people's participation in every sector of citizen's lives and implement the constitution in practice. From this analysis, the best conclusion is that Nepalese people got many things for the first time in history that should be sustainable to reconcile Nepalese politics in a post-conflict country like Nepal. If the political leaders of Nepal work to lead the country toward economic development, the model of peace process could serve as an asset for other countries that have experienced prolonged political conflict. The rise of Communists in Nepal and their support for communist ideology aim to prevent future conflicts. However, Nepali people have endured a long political transition and Nepalese political parties failed to bring the peace process into a logical conclusion risks plunging the country back into a dark future. The rise of the Communists in Nepal during the 2017 elections positioned them as a mainstream political actor, with the expectation of governing for five years by a single political party. Voting for the communists was perhaps a means for political stability and economic prosperity aligning with the promises made by the Left Alliance UML-Maoists before the elections. However, the current communist movement in Nepal is in crisis and to avoid this political dilemma the Maoist Center and UML are likely to unite.

NOTES

1. Welpton, *A History of Nepal*, xi.
2. Singh, 'Rise and Growth of Anti Rana Movement in Nepal', 992.
3. First political party of Nepal established to overthrow the Rana regime.
4. The first political party of Nepal.
5. Thapa and Sijapati, *A Kingdom under Siege: Nepal's Maoist Insurgency, 1990 to 2004*, 14.
6. Welpton, *A History of Nepal*, xii.
7. Victory to the cause of Sanskrit.
8. *Snellinger, Making New Nepal: From Student Activism to Mainstream Politics*, 35-6.
9. Welpton, *A History of Nepal*, 86.
10. Hachhethu, *Party Building in Nepal*, 1.
11. Ibid., 1.
12. Brown, *The Rise and the Fall of Communism*, 9.
13. Hachhethu, *Party Building in Nepal*, 1.
14. Nepal's Cabinet is Ousted by King; Mahendra Seizes Ministers as 'Anti-Nationalists' and Dissolves Parliament. *The New York Times*, 16 December 1960.
15. *Constitution of Nepal*, 1962.

16. King Tribhuvan was committed to hold the election for Constituent Assembly to draft the Constitution but died in 1954.
17. Grimond, *Splitting Image*, 29.
18. Malla, 'The Intellectual in Nepalese Society', 227.
19. Siwakoti, ed., *Democracy and Socialism: Thoughts of BP Koirala*, 197-8.
20. Karki and Seddon, *The People's War in Nepal: Left Perspectives*, 6.
21. *Constitution of Nepal, 2015.*
22. The supporters of *Panchayat* system are called *panchas.*
23. Tiwari, *1985 Yearbook on International Communist Affairs*, 220.
24. Lamsal, *Ideological Deviation in Politics.*
25. Brown, *The Rise and Fall of Communism*, 9.
26. Before 1990 NC and the parties included under the banner of United Left Forum agreed to established constitutional democracy. In the same time radical communist parties involved in UNPM had demanded republican system in Nepal.
27. Hutt, 'Drafting the 1990 Constitution', 32.
28. Hoftun, Raeper and Whelpton, *People, Politics and Ideology*, 134.
29. Baral, 'Nepal Political Parties and Parliament', 36.
30. Huntington, 'Democracy for the Long Haul', 67.
31. Sapkota, *Ten Years of Upheaval*, 15.
32. Shrestha, *Short History of Communist Movement in Nepal*, 37-8.
33. Thapa and Sijapati, *A Kingdom under Siege: Nepal's Maoist Insurgency, 1990 to 2004*, 34.
34. CPN (Mashal) was changed into CPN (Unity Center) in 1991 and finally it renamed as CPN (Maoist).
35. Nickson, 'Democratization and the Growth of Communism in Nepal: A Peruvian Scenario in the Making', 15.
36. Seven Political Parties and Nepal Communist Party (Maoist) agreed that the National Army and the Maoist Army would be under the supervision of the UN to conduct fair elections of CA and to accept international mediation.
37. Ministry of Foreign Affair, Kathmandu.
38. Ibid.
39. A conflict between landowners and tenants was announced by then King Mahendra in 1964. The Jhapa Rebellion was a peasant uprising that took place in the Jhapa district of Nepal in 1969.
40. Giri, 'A Leap of Six Decades', 20-5.
41. Lenin, *Left-Wing Communism: An Infantile Disorder.*
42. Thapa and Sijapati, *A Kingdom under Siege: Nepal's Maoist Insurgency,* 1990 to 2004.

43. Giri, 'A Leap of Six Decades', 20-5.
44. Khadka, 'Factionalism in the Communist Movement in Nepal'.
45. Tiwari, *1985 Yearbook on International Communist Affairs*, 246.
46. Sapkota, *Ten Years of Upheaval*, 234-5.
47. Ian Martin, 'The United Nations Support to Nepal's Peace Process: The Role of the UN Mission in Nepal', 205.
48. *Constitution of Nepal*, 2015.
49. Adhikari, *The Bullet and the Ballot Box: The Story of Nepal's Maoist Revolution*, xii.

REFERENCES

Adhikari, Aditya (2014), *The Bullet and the Ballot Box: The Story of Nepal's Maoist Revolution.* New Delhi: Rupa Publication.

Baral, Lok Raj (2004), 'Nepal Political Parties and Parliament.' In *The Unclear Roadmap: Parties and the Parliamentary Process.* New Delhi: Adroit Publications.

—— (2007), 'Prachanda on Prachanda Doctrine.' *The Kathmandu Post*, 9 May.

Brown, Archie (2009), *The Rise and Fall of Communism.* New York: Harper Collins.

Constitution of Nepal (1962), *Kathmandu, Nepal.*

Constitution of Nepal (2015), Kathmandu: Government of Nepal.

De Sales, A. (2000), 'The Kham Magar Country, Nepal: Between Ethnic Claims and Maoism'. *European Bulletin of Himalayan Research*, 19, Autumn, pp. 1-24.

Giri, Pradip. 'A Leap of Six Decades'. Nepal: *National Daily*, 2013.

Gupta, Bikash (2021), '*One Hat To Rule Them All: The Dhaka Topi And The Subjugation Of Minority Cultures In Nepal'.* www.recordnepal.com, Retrieved 1 July 2021.

Grimond, John (2015), 'Splitting Images,' *The Economist, The World in 2015.*

Hachhethu, Krishna (2002), *Party Building in Nepal: Organization, Leadership and People.* Kathmandu: Mandala Book Point.

—— (2006), 'Political Parties of Nepal', *Social Science Baha.* Retrieved on 11 June 2018.www.soscbaha.org/book/fbook/.../88.

—— (2009), The CPN (Maoist): Transformation from an Insurgency Group to a Competitive Political Party, *EBHR*, 33-34: pp. 39-71.

Hoftun, Martin, William Raeper and John Whelpton (1999). *People, Politics and Ideology.* Kathmandu: Mandala Book Point.

Huntington, Samuel (1996), 'Democracy for the Long Haul.' *Journal of Democracy.*

Hutt, Michael (2001), 'Drafting the 1990 Constitution', *Nepal in the Nineties.* New Delhi: Oxford University Press, 2001.

Karki, Arjun and David Seddon, eds. (2003), *The People's War in Nepal: Left Perspectives.* New Delhi: Adroit Publications.

Khadka, Narayan (1995), Factionalism in the Communist Movement in Nepal, *Pacific Affairs, University of British Columbia,* vol. 68, no. 1: pp. 55-76.

Lamsal, Yuba Nath (2017), *Ideological Deviation in Politics.* Retrieved on 12 June 2018. http://therisingnepal.org.np/news/14941.

Lenin, V. (1920). *Left-Wing Communism: An Infantile Disorder.* London.

Malla, K.P. (1973), 'The Intellectual in Nepalese Society.' *Nepal in Prosperity,* ed. Pashupati Shamser Rana and Kamal Prakash Malla. Kathmandu: CEDA, 263-90.

Martin, Ian (2012), 'The United Nations Support to Nepal's Peace Process: The Role of the UN Mission in Nepal'. In *Nepal in Transition: From People's War to Fragile Peace,* Eds. S.V. Einsidel, D.M. Malone and S. Pradhan. Cambridge: Cambridge University Press, 2012.

Nickson, R. Andrew (1992), 'Democratisation and the Growth of Communism in Nepal: A Peruvian Scenario in the Making?' *Journal of Commonwealth and Comparative Politics,* vol. 30, no. 3: pp. 358-86.

Rana, Pramode Shamshere J.B. (1999), *A Chronicle of Rana Rule.* Michigan: The University of Michigan.

Sapkota, Dipak (2010), *Ten Years of Upheaval: Reportage of the Decade Long Maoist People's War in Nepal.* Kathmandu: Revolutionary Journalist Association.

Shrestha, Puspalal (1997), *Short History of Communist Movement in Nepal.* Kathmandu: Puspalal Memorial Academy.

Singh, Chandra Prasad Singh (2004), 'Rise and Growth of Anti Rana Movement in Nepal', *Jostor,* vol. 65: pp. 992-1002.

Siwakoti, M.P. (ed.) (2022), Democracy and Socialism: Thoughts of B.P. Koirala. Kathmandu: Madhuvan Publication.

Snellinger, Amanda Therese (2018), *Making New Nepal: From Student Activism to Mainstream Politics.* Washington: University of Washington Press.

Spiess, Clemens (2009), *Democracy and Party Systems in Developing Countries: A Comparative Study of India and South Africa,* London: Routledge.

Thapa, Deepak & Bandita Sijapati (2006), *A Kingdom under Siege: Nepal's Maoist Insurgency, 1996 to 2003.* Kathmandu: The Print House.

Tiwari, C.K. (1985), *1985 Yearbook on International Communist Affairs,* Ed. Richard F. Staar, California: Hoover Institution Press.

—— (1989), *1989 Yearbook on International Communist Affairs*, Ed. Richard F. Staar, Hoover Institution Press, California.

Whelpton, John (2005), *A History of Nepal*. Cambridge: Cambridge University Press.

Wild, Leni Wild & Jiwan Subedi (2010), 'Review of International Assistance to Political Party and Party System Development: Case Study Report—Nepal' London: Overseas Development Institute. Retrieved on 6 June 2018 https://www.odi.org/sites/odi.org.uk/files/odi-assets/publications-opinion-files/6873.pdf

CHAPTER 2

Post-Conflict Political Participation of Women in Nepal

SARMILA BAGALE

HISTORICAL OVERVIEW OF NEPALESE WOMEN

The total population of Nepal as of 2021 was 29,164,578, with females comprising 51.13 per cent, which is slightly higher than the number of males.[1] The present Constitution of Nepal 2015 AD has guaranteed some specific provisions to offer certain political rights to women. It has acknowledged, 'Every woman shall have equal lineage right without gender-based discrimination', Article 38 and Article 38(5) accepts that [Nepalese] women have obtained special privileges in education, health, employment, social security, etc., to empower the women for making positive changes in their lives.[2]

Historically, Nepal, a Himalayan country, emerged as a unified state, the Kingdom of Gorkha Shah dynasty, which governed the Kathmandu valley. This region has a long history, with over 2,000 years of civilization. From the beginning to the emerging Shah dynasty, there was a very strong influence of Hindu patriarchal mindset in the Nepalese political system that continuously marginalized the women in the political system. Nepal is a culturally diverse country and Hindu religion played a significant role in shaping Nepalese society; and only the promulgation of Interim Constitution in 2006 changed in this provision.[3] In a patriarchal society, like Nepal, the relationship between male and female is formed by religious ideologies.[4] Hinduism has been a way of life for Nepalese people as majority of people follow this religion. It shapes the socio-cultural values in Nepalese society. R. Stump (2008) asserts that religion is deeply ingrained in peoples' experiences and behaviours which stimulates the socio-economic and political dynamics of societies.[5] In both the modern Western worldview, and in Nepal, religion shapes human perspective and influences the control of societal events.

Different perspectives of religion play a dominant role in shaping social system, e.g. substantive view of religion entails it as a system of culturally experiencing the way of life and its practices lean towards cultural dominion of people. The functional view of religion establishes powerful constant moods and motivations in people's mind to develop conceptions of a general order of existence. In this way, male domination in Nepalese society—despite the higher female population—is reflected in national policy. B.N. Adams and R.A. Sydie (2009) note that Western religion stems from a patriarchal worldview, resulting in patriarchal domination across all sectors.[6] In line with this, A. Sachedina (2003) remarked that women were historically denied fundamental human rights as a result of economic manipulation and exploitation of their position in the family and society.[7] Unlike this, the revolt of Yogmaya Neupane—a common Brahmin widowed-woman gave voices to the voiceless women, had married thrice when widow marriage was a deplorable offence in Nepalese society. It was an offence against religious values of Hindu socio-politico-cultural system that inspired Nepalese women to stand for their own future and fight against sexual discrimination. Her movement from traditional social beliefs to modern ways of thinking was an initiation of new threat to patriarchal political power system of Nepal.[8]

Michael Foucault (1981) states that the theoretical modality of political exclusion of women is a part of political ideas that intends to subordinate the females in social sector. For him, the notion of political exclusion of women leads to marginalization in socio-political sector. The emergence of exclusionary institutions is accompanied by the formation of scientific language that incorporates the idea of exclusion. He discusses exclusion and exclusionary procedures, whereby in every society the use of discourse is simultaneously managed, chosen, arranged and redistributed by a number of procedures whose purpose is to avoid its formidable, ponderous materiality, to gain control over its chance events and to fend off its powers and dangers.[9] S. Bem (1994) frameworks three elementary assumptions that shape the cultural understandings of human beings that make a difference between males and females. The hypotheses are 'andocentric', 'gender polarization' and 'biological essentialism'.[10] The androcentric assumption always places male at the centre and female at the periphery. The gender polarization reinforces the idea that male and female are socially different while biological essentialism is emphasized as the most important aspect of the society. In this context, the situation of women in Nepal is not different to other places and politics is a power device to shape and lead the society and other existing institutions for peace, participation and development. As everywhere, in Nepal women are holding less political power compared to their male counterparts and have occupied less political space to govern the country. One of the major reasons behind it is a patriarchal mindset that has created structural discrimination against women to create socio-economic barrier which is part of the political system for the meaningful sharing of power for the women in politics.

Nepalese society has differently structured the gender relations, in which women are seen to be predominantly cooking, cleaning and rearing children. Nepalese women, as in most of the countries, had very pathetic and terrible life. They were living with double exploitation of class and gender. In addition, child marriage, polygamy and forced marriage were prevalent in Nepalese society. Punam Yadav has analysed the condition of Nepalese women from the perspective of social transformation and views that the social realities and religious beliefs construct the political framework.[11] Bourdieu and Nice elucidate how masculine domination influences the structures of the political system. The social world view is always perceived by males as market goods for women.[12] As we have argued here religious social structure is based on masculine world view which since long had curbed the political desire of

Nepalese women, since the state culture is viewed as a social structure ruled by male principles. To justify it, the fundamental myth creates an opposition between nature and culture, or more specifically, between nature's sexuality and society's sexuality. The act of anomie, which is performed next to the fountain, the epitome of the feminine and was instigated by the woman, the perverse seductress, who was naturally knowledgeable about matters of love, contrasts with the act of nomos, which is domesticated and domesticated, performed at the behest of man and adhering to the order of things, fundamental hierarchy of the social order and cosmic order.[13] R. Eyben (2010) describes political empowerment as 'people's capacity to influence policy, make demands and call to account the state institutions that impact upon their lives. This includes political representation and collective action'.[14] In many public spheres and across all geographic regions, women continue to face severe discrimination because of their involvement in public and political life. The under representation of women in positions of authority and decision-making has many intricate and varied causes. In addition to negative stereotypes about women and ingrained gender roles, economic, social and cultural issues also pose significant barriers to women's involvement in public and political situations. The question of how gender is constituted differently in public and private spaces is central to the conceptualization of gender discrimination in the public domain. Feminist academics have been attempting to eliminate the barrier between public and private space for more than twenty years.[15]

WOMEN AFTER 1951 TO 1996

Two expected and highly ambitious plans were framed after the downfall of Rana regime that had ruled Nepal for 104 years. Deepak Thapa and Bandita Sijapati (2006) assert that King Tribhuvan had given a historic speech on 18 February 1951 and the monarch had declared his intention and choice to draft a democratic constitution by a constituent assembly.[16] This political shift of 1951 was a major political movement in Nepalese political history to protect the rights of the people in different fields. Even after the end of Rana regime, during the first democratic period (1951-61), the socio-political sphere of women in Nepal was not remarkably good and authoritative patriarchal domination still played in their lives. Women's political participation and inclusion in policy making level even in *Panchayat* regime (1961-90)[17] remained too thin and this non-democratic system could not bring any policy to change in the existing system. It failed to draw the devotion to macro policies of development for women's participation in politics and economic sectors. The political game of exclusion was practiced again, often in these same places and for the same reason—to make women weaker in politics and social sectors.

The *Panchayat* system had institutionalized the privileges of Kathmandu-elites that only prioritized the patriarchal system and ultimately it had marginalized the women. In Nepalese political history, the cultural understanding of male and female is different and is constructed by religious ideologies. Religious and cultural factors had placed the males at the centre and as Yadav writes until 2006 Hinduism was a dominant religious ideology in Nepal[18] and only the Interim Constitution 2007 had accepted Nepal as a secular country. The political movement of 1990 was an end of *Panchayat* system that reinstated a multi-party democratic system and brought a little change in political ideology. However, the new Constitution in 1991 failed to address the political problems of Nepalese women and they felt no substantial changes in their political career. It failed to make a good progress on people's participation in structural politics of Nepal. Catinca Slavu (2012) views that the failure of social inclusion to a large extent was a consequence of insufficient changes in the 1991 constitution and it maintained key exclusionary features reaffirming Nepal as a Hindu state and maintaining highly centralized state structures.[19] It had created a gap between the constitution, rhetoric and gender equality within Nepalese politics. The 1991 Constitution of the Kingdom of Nepal, called for the political parties to reserve at least 5 per cent candidature for women and made the assurance of 5 per cent women's representation in parliamentary system. The following subsequent national elections in 1991, 1994 and

1999 resulted in only 5 per cent and 6 per cent and 9 per cent of women's representation in parliament through election. These figures demonstrate women's representation in parliament increased on average by only 4 per cent.[20]

B.R. Upreti (2008) states that 'with the success of the democratic struggle of 1990, political awareness among Nepalese people had increased tremendously and their expectations with new government were much higher than in the past. However, the government failed to introduce good policies to fulfil the commitments'[21] and Yadav adds that the Government of Nepal slackened to bridge the gap between haves and have-nots and eliminating inequality based on caste, ethnicity, gender, religion, region and sex which encouraged the Maoists to lead the new movement for establishing new social system based on their leftist ideology.[22] The basic feature of women in democratic system of governance, even after the political changes of 1991, their participation and access to policy-making level was quite negligible. The Fourth World Conference on Women, held in Beijing in 1995 had focused on women's participation in all the decision-making levels around the world. In Nepal, women's participation in legislative, judiciary and executive were not felt important. It has thus become difficult for women to break from the vicious circle of poverty and disempowerment. Women were economically and politically disadvantaged due to their exclusion from the public domain and lack of public involvement.

Unlike this, Tulsi Acharya (2017) assumes that, after avoiding the constitution of 1991 by Maoists, Nepalese women's participation in political movements made them politically, socially and culturally conscious. It acknowledged the changes in their traditional ways of thinking to move ahead in the political history. Their encouraging participation in the political movement persuaded them to challenge the social, cultural and religious practices that had marginalized them for centuries. Once more, the study indicates that women's access to positions of political and administrative decision-making has been limited because of social expectations regarding their exclusive household responsibilities, limited mobility relative to men and limited access to economic and educational resources. The women's movement in Nepal after 1990 is shaped by many political forces and ideological perspectives and is ingrained in the country's political history. The constitution of 1990 had opined that 'Nepal is a multi-ethnic, multi-lingual, democratic, independent, sovereign, Hindu, constitutional, monarchical kingdom' and guaranteed fundamental rights to all citizens without discrimination based on ethnicity, caste, religion or sex.[23]

The political leaders had openly expressed the constitution to be 'the best constitution in the world'. However, the constitution had offered the king as the central authority and finally the constitution failed to incorporate many demands of common people, women, etc. A unified women's movement cannot emerge in a society that is driven by other hierarchical distinctions; it can only do so in tandem with the removal of other social bases of subordination aside from gender, despite the need for one being so obvious. This is why the most common catchphrase among Nepalese women activists even today is the lack of a certain political understanding. Secondly, attempts to enhance women's status via associations and campaigns that are inexorably influenced by other societal divisions could unintentionally or intentionally hinder the development of a cohesive women's movement.[24] Therefore, Nepalese women had realized the importance of power politics and got the ideas of power and its legitimacy in politics that had reshaped their mind to build the ideas of political authority. Without getting political power, social transformation for Nepalese women was not possible.

NEPALESE WOMEN IN CONFLICT

The failure of the constitution of Nepal was the basic point for the Maoists to wage a decade long conflict. They began the protest in 1996 and many women from rural area were involved in the rebellion. The women, then, played the roles in the militia, cultural group, joined to play active role in the Maoists' army and in the political wing of the party. They got actively involved in politics to get their political rights. Women mostly followed Marxism,

Leninism and Maoism (MLM) ideology, which in turn inspired them to be fully free from patriarchal domination. Before 1996, there was a growing recognition of political discrimination against women based on gender, class, and sex. In fact, there was a strong desire for social transformation across the regions of the country to permanently improve the condition of women. The CPN (Maoist) had expressed its firm commitment about ending patriarchal exploitation and gender discrimination and giving the right of granting parental property to daughters.[25] Similarly, Sierra Tamang agrees that among the many actors in the women's movement in Nepal after 1990s, the CPN-M has received the most attention. The majority of writing about the 'People's War' in Nepal by foreign and domestic journalists has included images of young and armed guerrilla women, wearing combat fatigues along with claims that between 30 per cent and 50 per cent of women participated in the conflict.[26] Hisila Yami (2007) concedes that the strategy of incorporating women into the people's army from the beginning has raised socio-political awareness, forcing the political parties of Nepal to recognize the need of addressing women's political demands which highlights the unique nature of the People's War.

The socio-political position of Nepalese women was shaped by political structure of the country which was prevalent at a political and socio-cultural level. The fundamental problems which have exploited the women as the second type of citizen was reflected in the context of Nepalese politics before the initiation of Maoist's movement were stronger than at present time were the exploitation in social sector and marginalization. Nepalese cultural imperialism and violence were of the same patriarchal domination. Before 1996 the women who had ideological influence of MLM had observed much discrimination and involvement in politics to get political freedom. In a short time, as Sharma and Prasain (2004) write that the number of Maoists cadres gradually increased to 30 per cent to 40 per cent, attracting common people. They affirm that women have taken up a variety of roles, including those of nurses, couriers, organizers and even fully-fledged guerrilla combatants.[27] The scholars have written that the women involved in Maoist movement were radical and CPN (Maoist) always advocated assuring rights for women, especially the working-class women. Yami (2006) writes Nepalese women became professionals in the revolution by joining People's Liberation Army, militias and production brigades. Women were instructed to target the feudal state apparatus as a means of combating class and gender oppression following the start of the Maoist struggle. For the first time, they were actively organized in villages against the landlord, patriarchal customs, superstitions and socio-cultural stigmata.

This political movement of 2006 gave women political power to make choices and guaranteed them a crucial role in legislature after the initiation of the peace process. Nepalese women were essential political and cultural activists throughout a ten-year political battle. They had even participated in the military operations of the rebels. Women who were family members of the security forces' were slained, raped, tortured and imprisoned throughout the fighting. The battle caused immense suffering to the spouses, mothers and daughters of men who were slained, disappeared, or subjected to torture. In addition to providing for their families' needs, they also had to fulfil social and economic obligations. Some women were involved in combat as well. From a philosophical perspective, the ten-year conflict in Nepal is seen as a catalyst for the socio-political inclusion of women, initiating structural changes within the political strata. This shift has transformed the concept of political realization into an understanding of the historical systems of political guidelines. In this regard, the Maoist movement in Nepal represented a significant political turn for bringing equality of women across social classes while advancing their professional and political prospects. It truly brought major changes in political and economic sectors for women, assisting in their empowerment in Nepal.

The Interim Constitution of Nepal (2007) sufficiently addressed gender and women's rights and, for the first time in Nepal's political history, recognized women as equal citizens to men. This legal provision brought significant changes, supporting women's empowerment and increasing their political participation in Nepalese politics. Regarding 'Citizenship', the Interim Constitution of Nepal (2007) approved the following provisions: no sex discrimination; employment and social security rights; women's rights; right to social justice; right against exploitation; and equality between men and women. The Constitution of 2015 reaffirms this in Article (11)(2)(b) stating that a person whose father or mother was a citizen of Nepal at their birth is entitled to citizenship by descent. This marked the first-time women were empowered in this way. However, as Susan Risal writes in *The Himalayan*, a major English newspaper, women wounded by conflict are battling both external and internal traumas. To help them mend their wounds and rehabilitate them in society with dignity, the state and the transitional justice systems must put in an effort. These women deserve justice, but they also deserve to live honourable lives. Despite these facts, the Interim Constitution incorporated some specific provisions to provide political support to women. The government set up provisions for women's political participation and constitutionalized it. Women's participation in politics through election processes to carry out the Constitution and their growing voice is marked and the 'yes we can do', mentality is predicted to contribute to equality and success in the economy as well. Empowerment analysis must consider women's engagement in public and political life in addition to their access to and mobilization within official and informal political venues. Political empowerment is no longer limited to the official sphere, which includes political parties and elections. It now faces additional obstacles as it must operate in entirely uncharted public and political areas regarding the strength of regional to international alliances, the voices and influence of women and innovative approaches to accountability. This paper sheds light on the ways in which the formal and informal converge, emphasizing these novel perspectives on public and political life and demonstrating how state-society connections might generate avenues for the advancement of gender equality objectives.

WOMEN IN POST-CONFLICT NEPAL

The initiation of peace process and promulgation of Interim Constitution were the consequences of a decade long conflict and the peaceful political movement of 2006. The first historic election of the Constituent Assembly in 2008 brought significant change in the pattern of gender equality. Women's representation in the Legislature Parliament increased dramatically to 33 per cent placing Nepal sixteenth out of 140 countries in terms of the percentage of women in national parliament, down from sixty-eight in 1999. According to Tamang Sierra, the people's movement of April 2006 exerted unprecedented pressure on the re-established parliament through the large-scale participation of women from excluded populations from urban to rural areas.[28] The most positive part of Nepali peace process that was framed after 2006 had accepted the principle of socio-political transformation of Nepalese people including women. It was against traditional thinking that had aimed to liberate Nepalese women from age long traditional method of production and way of life. In Schlitz's views a traditional society always accepts traditional values while a modern political world view always accepts the capacity of changing the society, inclusion of women in politics and finally making social transformation for peace and sustainable development. Nepalese Civil War that lasted for a decade was followed by the initiation of peace process and the election for the Constituent Assembly for drafting a constitution for Nepalese people. 32.8 per cent of Nepali women were elected as legislators in the voting system in 2008, which included a proportional system. This represents a significant improvement above the 5.8 per cent of women elected in 1999. According to K. Bhattarai and D. Budd (2008), Nepal became the region's leader in female representation overnight when one-third of the elected parliamentarians were female.[29]

The Constitution of Nepal 2015 aims to end 'all forms of discrimination and oppression created by the feudalistic, autocratic, centralized, unitary system of governance'[30] (Preamble) and it accepts the role of the glorious history of historic people's movements, armed conflict, dedication and sacrifice undertaken by Nepalese people that ensures political participation to ensure economic equality, prosperity and social justice for all people. Sarmila Bagale notes that women's empowerment is demonstrated by their election-based entry into politics for the purpose of enforcing the constitution and by the ensuing attitude of 'we can do it' that permeates contemporary society. It is anticipated that women who were marginalized before the adoption of the constitution 2015 will take a more active part in the growth and prosperity of the nation.[31] From this background, we can assume that Nepal has made significant progress on women's rights and political participation.

The academic research works available mainly in this sector focus on political and socio-economic transformation of Nepalese women. Jeevan Raj Sharma and Antonio Donini (2010) view that there is clear evidence of qualitative changes on the aspects of women's lives which seem more powerful than the normal process of change. They also believe that the current transition process is bringing about significant changes in important political, economic and sociocultural relationships. While the Maoists have played a major role in this process, other elements also significantly contributed to it.[32] Yadav (2016) opines the following remarks on the achievement of present constitution of Nepal as it is also explicitly stated in the 2015 that the women would not face any form of gender-based discrimination. Women now have equal rights over inheritance, protection from gender-based violence and reproductive health under the new constitution.[33] The political movement with specific guideline can have some intended results as Nepalese women got from the conflict of Nepal. In fact, the political movement which was followed by a successful peace process, led to structural changes by creating an enabling environment for women to exercise their political power. Women politics in Nepal moved from the hard conditions of civil conflict, women demonstration and transformation. In line with this, the conflict of Nepal had ultimately brought many positives changes especially for women. The representation of women in the first and second constituent assembly was a historic representation.

The present constitution of Nepal has given sufficient space to women in political and decision-making level and in the future, it will increase their capacity to fight for equality and justice. Again, it will by design reduce women's socio-economic and cultural vulnerability from Nepalese society. The access of Nepalese women in political field through electoral process can increase their representation in practice. The many women in numbers can participate in political level; it becomes easier to implement the constitution of Nepal. The positive attitude of women and their voice 'yes we can do' attitude has grown among the women is a good sign for women's political movement and it will enhance the prosperity and equality in politico-economic sector as well. The wave of a political conflict and the mass political movement heralded in the drafting of a new Constitution that ended a decade long political violent of Nepal. Offering the right to gender equality as a fundamental principle is one obvious tendency in this process of constitutional amendment. Realizing gender equality and allowing women to participate in politics is a standard of contemporary political values that protects each citizen's human rights. In the twenty-first century, widely accepted view is the inclusion of rights of women in which the women can enjoy democratic legitimacy and they feel they are the product of some process of public participation that reflects the composition of the population.

The 2017 local election was significant for women's political representation in Nepal. At least 40.4 per cent had to be nominated by the political parties in 753 local units. Of these 35,041 elected representatives, 40.96 per cent women got victory and in the political history of Nepal it was a great achievement.[34] In the case of national election held for Federal legislature parliament, in South Asian countries, Nepal tops the index of women in political participation which is the significant result of the political shift of inclusive democracy of Nepal.[35] The 2015 Nepalese Constitution recognizes that everyone has the right to live in dignity and guarantees 33 per cent of women equal representation in all political spheres. It also eliminates discrimination based on class, caste, sex, gender and other categories. The constitutional allowance of women to hold positions of political and decision-making authority would undoubtedly lessen the socioeconomic and cultural vulnerabilities that women face in Nepalese society. Women's participation in politics through election processes to carry out the Constitution and their growing 'yes we can do' mentality are predicted to contribute to equality and success in the economy as well.

CONCLUSION

The constitution looks at women's official political participation, such as their ability to choose political leadership roles, take part in politics and influence the political process after being elected. The advancements in these three areas of political participation of women since 2015 seems positive. It draws attention to national trends and advancements as well as obstacles preventing women from participating in the politics. In doing so, it examines efforts to demonstrate that, while political quotas are prevalent, there is the overwhelming evidence of their successful implementation. The women's advocacy movement is important because it has the potential to advance gender equality and drive change. When considering practical strategies, it is important to ensure that, once elected, women have a meaningful influence on decision-making and resource allocation.

In addition, political philosophy of every party is the main concern for the participation of women in response to the crisis of the modern republican country Nepal which has subsequently adopted the fundamental principles for the social model in the constitution. In such a case, it provides a philosophical discussion of inclusive democratic system and women can see the practice of political participation in national politics. Then, it creates a congenial environment between the legal and moral obligation of rights and questions the moral justifications offered for the right to inclusive political participation of women. For this, Nepalese Constitution acknowledges that all citizens shall be equal before law and in rights of women (Article 38) and it accepts that every woman shall have equal lineage right without gender-based discrimination and they have right to participate in all bodies of the State based on the principle of proportional inclusion.[36] If we observe the bright picture of women that the post-conflict constitution mirrors it seem positive and still there are some challenges in this sector. Due to educational background and political experiences compared to their male counterparts, women have inadequate political power to enjoy equal rights. For this, even at present the political role of all political parties seem to use the Constitutional rights to transform the socio-economic life of the women of Nepal. The status of women and their position in politics highlights some of the social and cultural issues with the country moving toward more women-friendly approaches. The study reflects the progress of women's status and their increasing political participation that can bring changes in modern society.

NOTES

1. National Population and Housing Census 2021.
2. The Constitution of Nepal, Articles 38 and 38(5).
3. Interim Constitution, Nepal.
4. WHR, *A Journal Towards Empowerment and Status of Single Women in Nepal*, 7.
5. Stump, *The Geography of Religion: Faith, Place and Space.*
6. Adams and Sydie, *Sociological Theory*, 276.
7. Sachedina, 'Globalization, Religion and Women', 11.
8. Yogmaya is also credited with founding the *Nari Samiti*, the first Nepali women's organization, in 1918. This group was the driving force for Nepal's 1920 decision to abolish the *Sati Pratha* (Aziz, 1993).
9. Foucault, 'The Order of Discourse', 210.
10. Bem, *In the Lenses of Gender: Transforming the Debate on Sexual Inequality.*
11. Yadav, *Social Transformation in Post-Conflict Nepal: A Gender Perspective*, 30.
12. Bourdieu, *Masculine Domination*, 99.
13. Ibid.
14. Eyben, 'Supporting Inclusive and Democratic Ownership. A "How to Note" for Donors'.
15. MacKinnon, *Toward a Feminist Theory of the State.*
16. Thapa and Sijapati, 2006, 15.
17. Partyless political system introduced by King Mahendra that lasted for 30 years.
18. Yadav, *Social Transformation in Post-Conflict Nepal: A Gender Perspective*, 2016, 37.
19. Slavu, 'The 2008 Constituent Assembly Election: Social Inclusion for Peace', 235.
20. Report on Gender Mapping in the Field of Elections, 2.
21. Upreti, 'Resistance Movement in Conflict Transformation and Social Change', 2008, 37.

22. Yadav, *Social Transformation in Post-Conflict Nepal: A Gender Perspective.*
23. The Constitution of the Kingdom of Nepal 1990.
24. Des Chene, 'Nepali Women's Movement: Experiences, Critiques, Commentaries', 294.
25. The forty-point charter, which is included in 19, was submitted to the government of Nepal in 1996 by CPN (Maoist).
26. Tamang, 'The Politics of Conflict and Difference of Conflict in Politics: The Women's Movement in Nepal', 73.
27. Sharma and Prasain, 'Gender Dimensions of the People's War: Some Reflections on the Experiences of Rural Women', 152.
28. Women in National Parliaments—www.ipu.org, 26 April.
29. Bhattarai and Budd (2008). 'Political Parties in Nepal: Opportunities and Challenges', 75-88.
30. Preamble of the Constitution of Nepal, 2015.
31. Bagale, 'Participation of Nepali Women in Politics'.
32. Sharma and Donini, 'Towards a Great Transformation: The Maoist Insurgency and Local Perceptions of Social Transformation in Nepal', 20.
33. Yadav, *Social Transformation in Post-Conflict Nepal: A Gender Perspective*, 52.
34. Nepal's Locally Elected Women Representatives: Exploratory Study of Needs and Capacity, 6.
35. Shekhawat 'Women in parliament: Nepal top, Bangladesh 4th in South Asia'. According to data released by Inter-Parliamentary Union, Nepal ranks first, Afghanistan ranks second, Pakistan third, Bangladesh fourth, India fifth, Bhutan sixth, Maldives seventh and Sri Lanka obtains eighth position in SAARC region.
36. Article 38(4) of the Constitution of Nepal, 2015.

REFERENCES

Acharya, Tulasi, 'Nepal Himalaya: Women, Politics and Administration', *Journal of International Women's Studies*, vol. 18, no. 4, 2017. Retrieved on 5 July 2018 http://vc.bridgew.edu/cgi/viewcontent.cgi?article=1972&context=jiws.

Adams, B.N. and Sydie, R.A. (2009). *Sociological Theory.* New Delhi: Vanisagar Publication.

Aziz, Barbara Nimri (1993). *Shakti Yogmaya: A Tradition of Dissent in Nepal.* Kathmandu: Tribhuvan University.

Bagale, Sarmila. 'Participation of Nepali Women in Politics', *The Rising Nepal,* vol. LIII, no. 228, 2018. Retrieved on 5 June 2018 http://therisingnepal.org.np/news/24422.

Bem, S. (1994). *In the Lenses of Gender: Transforming the Debate on Sexual Inequality.* New Haven: Yale University Press.

Bennett, Lyn. (1983). *Dangerous Wives and Sacred Sisters.* New York: Columbia University Press.

Bhattarai, K. and Budd, D. (2008). Political Parties in Nepal: Opportunities and Challenges. *The Journal of the Institute of Justice & International Studies,* 8: 75-88.

Bourdieu, P. (2001). *Masculine Domination.* Cambridge: Cambridge Polity Press.

Des Chene, M. (1997) 'Nepali Women's Movement: Experiences, Critiques, Commentaries', *Studies in Nepali History and Society,* vol. 2, no. 2: 291-7.

Dhungana, Raj Kumar. 'Nepali Hindu Women's Thorny Path to Liberation', *Journal of Education and Research,* vol. 4, no. 1. 2014, Retrieved on 11 July 2018. http://oaji.net/articles/2017/6030-1519944455.pdf

Douglas, Mary (1970). *Natural Symbols: Explorations in Cosmology.* New York: Vintage.

Eyben, Rosalind (2010). 'Supporting Inclusive and Democratic Ownership. A "How to Note" for Donors. Institute of Development Studies.

Foucault, M. (1981). 'The Order of Discourse', R. Young (ed.), *Untying The Text: A Post-Structuralist Reader.* Boston: Routledge & Kegan Paul.

International Crisis Group (ICG) (2003). Nepal Backgrounder: Ceasefire-Soft Landing or Strategic Pause? Kathmandu/Brussels: ICG.

Jha, Bina (2015). 'Women in politics: Equal treatment is a must'. *The Himalayan Times.* https://thehimalayantimes.com/opinion/women-in-politics-equal-treatment-is-a-must/.

Lal, Abha. 'Revisiting revisionist history', *My Republica.* Retrieved on 16 July 2018. https://myrepublica.nagariknetwork.com/news/revisiting-revisionist-history/.

MacKinnon, Catharine. (1989). *Toward a Feminist Theory of the State,* Harvard University Press.

Marit, Haug and Aadne Aasland (2015). 'Exploring Dimensions of Women's Social Exclusion and Inclusion in Nepal'. Retrieved on 12 June 2018 https://www.tandfonline.com/doi/abs/10.1080/08039410.2015.1114517?journalCode=sfds20.

National Population and Housing Census 2021 (National Report).

Pradhan, Pratibha. 'The Status of Women in Political Participation in Nepal', *The Himalayan Review*. Retrieved on 10 July 2018. https://www.nepjol.info/index.php/HR/article/view/2415/2155

Risal, Susan. 'Conflict-hit women: Still far from justice', *The Himalayan*. Retrieved on 11 July 2018. https://thehimalayantimes.com/opinion/conflict-hit-women-still-far-from-justice/

Sachedina, A. (2003). 'Globalization, Religion and Women'. *Critical Half*, 1(1), 11-14.

Sharma, Jeevan Raj and Antonio Donini (2010). 'Towards a Great Transformation: The Maoist Insurgency and Local Perceptions of Social Transformation in Nepal', *Feinstein International Center*. Retrieved on 12 July 2018 http://fic.tufts.edu/assets/great-transformation.pdf.

Sharma, M. and Prasain, D. (2004). Gender Dimensions of the People's War: Some Reflections on the Experiences of Rural Women. *Himalayan 'People's War': Nepal's Maoist Rebellion*. Michael Hutt, ed., London: Hurst and Company, 152-65.

Slavu, Catinca (2012). 'The 2008 Constituent Assembly Election: Social Inclusion for Peace', *Nepal in Transition: From People's War to Fragile Peace*. Eds. Sebastian Von Einsiedel, David M. Malone & Suman Pradhan. New Delhi: Cambridge University Press.

Stiglitz, J. (1998). Towards a new Paradigm for Development: Strategies, Policies and Process. Retrieved on 1 August 2018. http://web.worldbank.org/archive/website01013/WEB/IMAGES/PREBISCH.PDF.

Stump, R. (2008). *The Geography of Religion: Faith, Place and Space*. Maryland: Rowman and Littlefield Publishers.

Tamang, Sierra (2009). The Politics of Conflict and Difference of Conflict in Politics: The Women's Movement in Nepal. *Feminist Review*, 91, 61-80.

Thapa, Deepak and Bandita Sijapati (2006). *A Kingdom Under Siege: Nepal's Maoist Insurgency, 1996 to 2004*. London/New York: Zed Books.

The Constitution of the Kingdom of Nepal, 1990, Kathmandu: Law Books Management Board.

The Interim Constitution of Nepal, 2007, Kathmandu: Law Books Management Board.

The Constitution of Nepal, 2015, The Government of Nepal: Law Books Management Board.

Upreti, B.R. (2008). 'Resistance Movement in Conflict Transformation and Social Change'. Kathmandu: Human and Natural Resource Center.

Whelpton, J. (2005). *A History of Nepal*. Cambridge: Cambridge University Press.

WHR (2010). *A Journal Towards Empowerment and Status of Single Women in Nepal.* Kathmandu.

Yadav, P. (2016). *Social Transformation in Post-Conflict Nepal: A Gender Perspective.* London: Routledge.

Yami, H. (2007). *People's War and Women's Liberation in Nepal.* Kathmandu: Janadhwani Publication.

CHAPTER 3

Empowering Crime Victims: Navigating Nepali Legal Framework

SHOVA PATHAK

INTRODUCTION

The traditional criminal justice system pays very little attention to the victims of crime. For Salmond the purpose of criminal justice is punishment. We can regard it as a method of protecting society by reducing the occurrence of criminal behaviour or else we can consider it as an end. Punishment can protect society deterring potential offender and by reforming and turning him into a law-abiding citizen.[1]

Not only criminal justice system of states but also the international law paid sufficient attention to crime victims. Carlos Fernandez de Casadevante Romani wrote, 'As it is well known and owing to the predominantly interstate structure of the international community, international norms are created to respond to states' interests and goal. In this context attention to persons or individuals by states has only taken place in some field of international law.'[2] According to him in case with human rights, international criminal law or international humanitarian law, the way in which the victims are considered differs.[3]

In human rights law, victims are acknowledged when the state is the author of the breach of an international obligation, but this branch of international law does not consider the breach of international obligations by non-state actors.[4] In international criminal law and international humanitarian law on the other hand individuals may be regarded as victims as a consequence of acts perpetrated by individuals as well as by non-state actors.[5] Therefore, international community has not yet codified binding international norms generally applicable to the victims of all types of crimes.

The victims have certain rights which must be protected to ensure that they get a fair treatment from the state agencies in the criminal justice process. Their concerns and needs must be responded sensitively by informing them about the progress of the case and by minimizing their miseries, offering protection and security to them and their families against any intimidation and retaliation. The police require the cooperation and support from the victim to prepare the case for prosecution in addition to tracing and apprehending the offender. Therefore, the protection of the crime victim is not only the protection offered to them but the protection of criminal justice and the whole justice system.

MEANING AND DEFINITION OF CRIME VICTIM

'Crime victim' is a person who has been physically, financially or emotionally injured and/or had their property taken or damaged by someone committing a crime. Traditionally, the term crime victim has been defined as an individual who has been directly subjected to criminal activity.[6] This definition of crime victim excludes the family members or defendant of the person who died because of crime. German criminologist Hans Joachim Schneider states that a victim can be an individual, an organization, 'the moral order' or the legal system of a state which is threatened, harmed, or destroyed by an action.[7] The Declaration of Basic Principles of Justice for Victims of Crime and Abuse of Power defines crime victim in the following words:

> 'Victims' means persons who, individually or collectively, have suffered harm, including physical or mental injury, emotional suffering, economic loss or substantial impairment of their fundamental rights, through acts or omissions that are in violation of criminal laws operative within Member States, including those laws proscribing criminal abuse of power.[8]

Crime Victim Protection Act, 2075 (2018) has provided three types of victims namely First Degree Victim, Second Degree Victim and Family Victim in the form of a natural person. First Degree Victim means a person who as a result of the offender's age, mental illness, diplomatic immunity or professional immunity does not have to bear criminal liability or the offender's identity is unknown or charge is not made against the offender or the case related to the crime is taken back or the punishment imposed to the offender is pardoned or conviction is not made or regardless of the relation between the victim and offender, death occurred as a direct result of the crime commit detains the victim or loss is suffered and the term shall also indicate the person who dies or suffers loss while not engaging in crime in any of the following conditions:

1. While acting to stop the person from committing the crime.
2. While acting to provide reasonable support and rescue, in conditions when crime is being committed against a person, with an objective to prevent such a person from crime.
3. While attempting to arrest a person who is committing or has committed a crime or while providing help to an authorized person in course of arresting a suspicious, accused or convicted person.

Likewise, 'Second Degree Victim' means a person who is not involved in the crime committed or being committed against the First Degree Victim but as a result of being an eyewitness incurred loss and this term shall also mean a person not involved in the crime but has information of the crime or a guardian of a First Degree Minor Victim who incurred loss as a result of being an eyewitness and the term shall also mean the following persons who incurred loss as a result of having knowledge of the crime committed against the First Degree Victim:

(i) Guardian of First Degree Victim,
(ii) in case the First Degree Victim is a minor, and
(iii) in case the person incurring such loss is not involved in such crime.

'Family Victim' means the mother, father, husband, wife in consanguinity with the dead victim or any other person in the consanguinity family dependent on the victim who is not involved in the crime committed against the First Degree Victim as a direct consequence of which he or she died.

VICTIM OF CRIME UNDER CRIMINAL JUSTICE SYSTEM

A justice system depends upon evidence against the case; they are appropriately being collected and presented before the courts. And, particularly, if fear prevails, collection of evidence is very difficult or not at all. The absence of evidence may finally lead to not taking up the cases or dismiss the charges against the accused, as the court can only consider on the matters brought before the court. This will lead to the space to weaken the case or escape the real culprits/perpetrators or lose the case.

Silencing victims through fear is one of the worst forms of impunity. It maintains the illusion of the rule of law and a legal system capable of following up wrongdoing. If any, complaints are made and if they are, they rarely result in prosecutions or convictions. Silence denies the existence of the problem; the problem may be known but is never spoken about.[9] One of the challenges for many countries is in obtaining the cooperation of victims and witnesses to obtain important information and evidence about the criminal matters.[10]

The Declaration of Basic Principles of Justice for Victims of Crime and Abuse of Power, 1985, recognizes four basic rights of crime victims as:

- The right of access to trial proceedings and fair treatment.
- The right to compensation by the perpetrator.
- The right to compensation by the state.
- The right to necessary material, medical, psychological and social assistance from volunteer and public institutions.

The Constitution of Nepal drafted by the Constituent Assembly has guaranteed the right of crime victim including right to justice and compensation, for the first time in the world. The statutes drafted thereafter including the Muluki Criminal Code, 2017 and Muluki Criminal Procedure Code, 2017 and the Sentencing Act, 2017 have incorporated important provisions regrading the right of crime victims. Recently, the parliament has enacted comprehensive law for the protection of crime victim in 2018. In the later sections, the provisions of national law regarding crime victims including constitutional provisions, the provisions of general laws and specific legal provisions on rights to crime victim will be discussed in detail.

CONCEPT OF RIGHTS OF VICTIMS OF CRIME

The word 'right' generally means a claim or an interest provided by the law or rights recognized and protected by law. The rights of crime victims mean the rights or claim of the victim of crime in the criminal justice process when they are a direct or an indirect victim. According to the US Code SS 3771(1) there are the following rights:

1. The right to be reasonably protected from the accused.
2. The right to reasonable, accurate and timely notice of any public court proceeding, or any parole proceeding, involving the crime or of any release or escape of the accused.
3. The right not to be excluded from any such public court proceeding, unless the court, after receiving clear and convincing evidence, determines that testimony by the victim would be materially altered if the victim hears other testimony at that proceeding.
4. The right to be reasonably heard at any public proceeding in the district court involving release, plea, sentencing or any parole proceeding.
5. The reasonable right to confer with the attorney for the Government in the case.
6. The right to full and timely restitution as provided in law.
7. The right to proceedings free from unreasonable delay.

8. The right to be treated with fairness and with respect for the victim's dignity and privacy.
9. The right to be informed in a timely manner of any plea bargain or deferred prosecution agreement.
10. The right to be informed of the rights under this section and the services described in section 503(c) of the Victims' Rights and Restitution Act of 1990 [42 U.S.C. 10607(c)]/[1] and provided contact information for the Office of the Victims' Rights Ombudsman of the Department of Justice.[11]

According to the Declaration of Basic Principles of Justice for Victims of Crime and Abuse of Power, 1985,

- The right of access to trial proceedings and fair treatment.
- The right to compensation by the perpetrator.
- The right to compensation by the state.
- The right to necessary material, medical, psychological and social assistance from volunteer and public institutions

The Right to Access to Justice and Fair Treatment

The crime victim thus receives the right to respect and acknowledgements at all levels of the criminal proceedings that is they have right to access the mechanism of justice and to prompt redress for the harm they have suffered. They have the right to receive continual information about how the case is proceeding, the right to give information to those responsible for decisions regarding the criminal, access to legal counsel, protection of personal integrity and physical security and the right to economic compensation.

Right to Restitution

Restitution means payment made to the victim for damage suffered because of crime. It is intended to repay victims for their losses caused by the crime. The Declaration on the Rights of Victim emphasized on the fair restitution to the victim of crime. According to the paragraph 8, offenders or third parties responsible for their behaviour should, where appropriate, make fair restitution to victims, their families or dependents. Such restitution should include the return of property or payment for the harm or loss suffered, reimbursement of expenses incurred because of the victimization, the provision of services and the restoration of rights.

Right to Compensation

It is the duty of the state to protect the life and property of people. The consequence of the state's failure should not be borne by the people. This matter has been recognized by the declaration. The declaration provides that when compensation is not fully available from the offender or other sources, States should endeavour to provide financial compensation to the victims who have sustained significant bodily injury or impairment of physical or mental health as a result of serious crimes; the family, in particular dependents of persons who have died or become physically or mentally incapacitated as a result of such victimization.

Right to Assistance

Crime victims require assistance in various aspects including medical, psychological and social assistance for their physical protection as well as for successful prosecution against the wrong-doer. According to paragraphs 14 to 17 of the declaration, the victims should receive the necessary material, medical, psychological and social assistance through governmental, voluntary, community-based and indigenous means. They should be informed of the availability of health and social services and other relevant assistance and be readily afforded access to them. Police, justice, health, social service and other personnel concerned should receive training to sensitize them to the needs of victims and guidelines to ensure proper and prompt aid. In providing services and assistance to victims, attention should be given to those who have special needs.

RIGHTS OF CRIME VICTIMS UNDER NEPALI LEGAL FRAMEWORK

CONSTITUTIONAL PROVISION ON THE RIGHTS OF CRIME VICTIMS

Nepali criminal justice system has taken a big leap in the protection of the rights of crime victim in recent years Constitution of Nepal made by the Constituent Assembly has guaranteed the right of the crime victim for the first time. Article 21 of the Constitutions under the Right of Victim of crime provides:[12]

Right of Victim of Crime: (1) A victim of crime shall have the right to get information about the investigation and proceedings of a case in which he or she is the victim.

(2) A victim of crime shall have the right to justice including social rehabilitation and compensation in accordance with law.

The Constitution of Nepal for the first time in the world has engraved the rights of the Crime Victim. The victim of crime not only has the right to get information regarding the investigation and proceeding of the case but also the right to justice including social rehabilitation and compensation in accordance with law. This constitutional provision has a wider connotation. According to this Constitutional provision the crime victim has the right to get information about the proceeding of the case at every step of criminal process from investigation to prosecution, trial, appeal and execution of the judgement. The investigating and prosecuting authorities as well as the court have the duty to inform the victim of the proceeding of the case. The crime victim also has the right to justice including social rehabilitation and compensation.

PROVISION OF GENERAL LAW REGARDING THE RIGHTS OF CRIME VICTIMS

There have been very few legal provisions regarding to the rights of crime victims before the commencement of this Act. These provisions have limited connotation and are limited only to some aspects of victim's right like protection of the victim, privacy and compensation. These provisions do not cover the most important aspect of right that is the right to access to justice. However, the statutes drafted after the commencement of the constitution, i.e. the Muluki Criminal Code, 2017 and Muluki Criminal Procedure Code, 2017 and the Sentencing Act, 2017 have incorporated important provisions regarding the right of crime victims.

The Human Trafficking and Transportation (Control) Act, 2007 has made some provision about the rights of crime victims including the protection of the confidentiality of the crime victim and right to compensation. 'Caste Based Discrimination and Untouchability (Offence and Punishment) Act, 2068 (2011)' has criminalized the act of discrimination and made provision for restitution to the victim. Likewise, the Children Act, 2018 has ensured various rights of child victims including the right to information the language he or she understands, to participate, right confidentiality, right to compensation from the offender as well as from State, right to free legal aid and socio-psychological counselling service, right to free service of the translator, sign language expert or interpreter, right to get free of cost, the copy of the documents including the decisions and orders, right to get police protection for safety against the probable.[13] Domestic Violence (Crime and Punishment) Act, 2066 (2009) offered for immediate protection of the victim and protecting her from further victimization,[14] provision of in camera proceedings and hearings of the complaint.[15] Motor Vehicles and Transport Management Act, 1993 has the provision of compensation and medical expense to be paid to the victim by the offender in case of loss of life, injury to body or loss of property.[16]

The codes relating to criminal justice including the Muluki Criminal Code, 2017, Muluki Criminal Procedure Code, 2017 and Sentencing Act, 2017 and rules thereof have been brought into commencement of the Constitution of Nepal in 2015. Section 32 of the Country Criminal Code guarantees the same right in the similar term under the title 'Victim of crime to be entitled to obtain information of proceedings of case and compensation'. Section 13(c) of the Criminal Offence (Determination and Execution of Sentence) Act, 2017 has provided that the court, while determining the sentence has to take into account of delivering justice along with compensation to the victim.[17]

Rights of the Crime Victim under Crime Victim Protection Act, 2018

Constitutional guarantee of the rights of crime victims and formulation of Crime Victim Protection Act, 2075 has been significant achievement in the field of rights of crime victims. The Act has classified victim as 'Victim of First Grade', 'Victim of Second Grade' and 'Family Victim' and made provision for providing compensation and relief. The rights guaranteed by the Act can be discussed under the following headings:

Right to Protection and Security

It is the foremost right of the victim to be protected from further victimization her/him and his/her family from the offender. Protection includes protection from attack, loss, fear, threat or intimidation that may be against the victim or the close relative of the victim and the person dependent on the victim from the suspected person, accused, convict or person related to the convict or the witness of accused.[18]

Right to Fair Treatment and Non-discrimination

Victim shall have the right to receive civilized, noble, fair and dignified treatment in criminal justice process.[19] Victim shall not be discriminated in the criminal justice process on the basis of his or her religion, race, sex, caste, ethnicity, gender, origin, language, marital status, family status, age, physical or mental illness, disability or ideology or such other basis.[20] However, the victims with the special needs like minor, elderly citizens or physically or mentally incapable persons have to be considered in the context of criminal justice process.

Right to Privacy

The Act has also guaranteed the victim of some sensitive crimes like rape, incest, human trafficking, sexual harassment, the right to privacy in the course of investigation, inquiry, prosecution and judicial proceedings.[21] If any deed and testimony or deputation has to be made in the course of investigation, inquiry and judicial proceedings of the crimes it has to be prepared by presenting victim in a way to not reveal his or her identity. It has to be made by changing the real voice of the victim. If video conference has to be made in a way the offender is unable to see or hear.

Right to Information Relating to Investigation

The investigation officer, prosecutors and the court have to provide information regarding the investigation, prosecution and court proceeding in the case. It enables the victim to know the progress of the case as well as take further step in protecting her interest and securing justice.

Right to Express Opinion[22]

The victim's right to express opinion about the process of making decision relating to prosecution, plea bargaining, mitigating the sentence, making additional charges, making pre-sentencing report, determining sentence and making decision regarding diversion, probation, parole, suspended sentence, open prison, community service or any other facilities of similar nature to the offender.[23]

Right to Participation

Another important right of the victim is the right to be present and make one's statement in the proceedings relating to the court hearing in relation to the crime.[24] The victim has the right to express opinion in the sentencing process also.

Right to Make Written Application or Appeal

The victim has the right to make a written application before the concerned agency or authority requesting for filing an application or appeal against the order of the court if Government of Nepal has the right to file an application or appeal against such order or decision of the court according to prevailing law.[25]

Right to Compensation

Right to receive compensation is another important right of the crime victim for realization of justice. Section 18 provides that if the victim is entitled to get compensation according to this Act or other prevailing law and if he/she requests for information about it the prosecuting authority should give information to the victim in relation to the procedures to be fulfilled relating to receiving compensation.[26] Section 19 of the Act provides that the victim shall have the right to receive compensation for the loss he/she suffered.[27]

Right to Stay in a Separate Chamber During the Hearing

In the course of the hearing of the offence, the court may provide a separate chamber for the victim so that he or she can stay separately from the accused, person related to the accused and witness of the accused.[28] If it is not possible to provide separate chamber make necessary arrangement for the safety and interest of the victim so that the accused, person related to the accused and witness of the accused cannot contact the victim, except as otherwise ordered by the court.

Right to Have Property Returned

The victim has the right to have his or her property taken under control during investigation or for evidence, returned immediately after the completion of investigation. However, if such property is to be submitted to the court for evidence or there is a dispute as to the ownership or possession of the property, the property shall not be returned before the dispute is settled. The court may, if it so thinks necessary, make an order to return such property before the dispute is settled.[29]

Right to Social Rehabilitation

Rehabilitation is a crucial right of the crime victim to enable him/ her live a normal life. The victim should be protected from further victimization and revictimization. It depends on the context, such measures range from external oversight and monitoring mechanisms to the establishment of judicial remedies, the strengthening of the judiciary's independence. The Act has a provision regarding social rehabilitation of the victim however, it has not defined what social means.

Interim Compensation

According to the Section 29 of the Act in case victim has to be immediately treated or if compensation or any form of relief amount has to be provided, the court may give order to conduct medical treatment or to provide interim form of compensation or relief for such person. Such compensation shall be provided from the Fund.

Right to Appoint Legal Practitioner

Right to access to justice includes the right to effective representation which is not possible without legal practitioner. Although, the prosecutor represents the victim in the court, the victim also has the right to representation with the help of a law practitioner. The Act ensures that crime victims have the right to appoint a separate legal practitioner in the criminal justice process if they wish.[30]

ROLE OF SUPREME COURT IN THE PROTECTION OF RIGHTS OF CRIME VICTIMS

The Supreme Court of Nepal has played an important role in the protection of the rights of victims of crime. It has taken a proactive approach in ensuring access to justice, safeguarding victims, and securing compensation and restitution for them. The Court's decisions and orders reflect its commitment to these vital protections.

Victim's Right to Access to Justice

The Supreme Court of Nepal has issued a landmark ruling in the case crime victim Suntali Dhami[31] reinforcing the protection of the right to access justice. The Court held that the malafide and arbitrary exercise of prosecutorial power is subject to judicial review. Likewise, Supreme Court in writ of mandamus of Punyashila Dawadi Ghimire *vs.* PMO[32] and others held that:

> The state, for purpose of making the access to justice easy has to adopt proper measures. The environment of realizing the care and protection of state by the victim has to be created. The state has to take measures to stop the barriers that discourage the women victim of rape and human trafficking from seeking judicial remedies and have been forced to live with mental, physical and psychological suffering.

The Supreme Court has made similar order in the writ of Certiorari and Mandamus of Jyoti Lamsal *vs.* GoN, PM and PMO[33] and in the writ of certiorari of Narayan Singh Rajpoot *vs.* Office of the Attorney General of Nepal.[34] In Narayan Singh Rajpoot case the Supreme Court held:

> There is the provision of police for carrying out investigation of crime and the government has also made the provision of Government Attorney to screen the evidence, prosecute and defend the case in the court on behalf of the victim.

The Supreme Court, then the writ of Mandamus of Meera Dhungana *vs.* PMO[35] issued a six-point directive to the respondents, instructing them to establish a plan to provide the victim with information about the investigation from the concerned police office. The directives also required the prosecutor to inform about the charges and court's judgement, including copies of the charge sheet and judgement.

Confidentiality of the Victim

Protection of the confidentiality of victim is directly connected with her physical protection. Supreme Court of Nepal has played very important role in the protection of confidentiality of victim. The Supreme Court, in a writ petition for Mandamus filed by Sapana Pradhan Malla, issued a directive order to the Government of Nepal, the Council of Ministers and the Ministry of Law and Justice to formulate laws for maintaining confidentiality in special types of cases involving women, children or individuals infected from HIV Aids, outlining the rights and responsibility of the concerned parties. The Court also issued directives consisting of 13 Sections to remain effective until such a law is formulated. In the order, the Supreme Court held that,[36] in the human trafficking case of Sunil Lama *vs.* GoN, it analysed the principle of victimology for the first time and concluded that:

> . . . the defendant alluring the victim of marrying her took to brothel of India and sold her. The victim got out of the life of hell of the brothel, lodged FIR and her statement has been certified from the court . . . the statement of the victim certified from the court is admissible as evidence even if she has not testified in the court.[37]

Supreme Court Approach Regarding Compensation

Compensation is essential for protecting and assisting victims of crime. The Supreme Court before the commencement of Crime Victim Protection Act, 2018 developed a procedure for compensating rape victims due to the absence of clear recovery procedure. In GoN *vs.* Swosti Baral, the Court held that it is the government's duty to claim compensation for the victim by ascertaining the defendant's property details and specifying the grounds and reasons for recovering the compensation in the charge sheet.[38] The Supreme Court in the rape case of Rakesh Kumar Singh *vs.* GoN[39] held that in rape cases the District Court has to give information to the victim after final judgement and execute the judgement as well as recover the compensation to the victim. This although, is not written in the law. The most significant and inspiring judgement regarding compensation to the victim is the ruling of the Court in Lok Bahadur Sharki et al. *vs.* GoN.[40] The Supreme Court held that:

> From now onwards, it is appropriate to provide compensation fixed by the final judgement of the court immediately to the victim of the crimes of such nature in which compensation is payable, by establishing a separate fund by the government and recover it from the offender as government due. Therefore, it is required to make necessary infrastructure by the government in this regard.

CONCLUSION

The new Constitution of Nepal has brought a paradigm shift in the role and status of victims in the criminal justice system. The Crime Victim Protection Act, 2018, has been enacted and implemented for translating these rights into practice. The Act has been implemented and the rights of crime victims have been safeguarded. A Victim Relief Fund has been established and a relief fee is levied from every convict in a criminal case. However, the situation of crime victim cannot change overnight, as it is not easy to implement new concepts in practice. The rights enshrined in the Constitution or laws must be put into practice through the collaborative efforts of all relevant stakeholders, which is a very challenging task. The government must manage this effectively. A clear understanding of the concept related to victims' right and protection measures is essential for safeguarding victims' right in every stage of the criminal justice procedure. To internationalize the concept of victim justice among key stakeholders, sensitization programmes should be carried out. Fundamentals of victim protection must be included in training course designed for judicial cadres, prosecutors, police investigators and defence lawyers. Additionally, a crime victim information mechanism should be established within police stations and public prosecutor offices to provide regular updates on the progress of their cases. Various legislations contain the provisions related to victim protection and compensation. Harmonization of these legal provisions is essential to ensure consistency in practice.

NOTES

1. P. J. Fitzerald, *Salmond on Jurisprudence,* 12th edn. (1966), N.M. Tripathee, Bombay, 94.
2. Carlos Farnandez de Casadevante Romani (2010), Max Plank UNYB14, p. 221.
3. Ibid.
4. Ibid.
5. Ibid.

6. Magnus Lindgren and Vesna Nikoliæ-Ristanoviæ (2011), *Crime Victims: International and Serbian Perspective,* Organization for Security and Constitution Cooperation in Europe, Mission to Serbia, Law Enforcement Department, 19.
7. Ibid.
8. Article 1(1) of The Declaration of Basic Principles of Justice for Victims of Crime and Abuse of Power, 1985.
9. V.G. Paulina and F. Carla (2009), 'Ending Threats and Reprisals Against Victims of Torture and Related International Crimes: A Call to Action, 6.
10. Kramer, K., (2010), 'Witness Protection as a Key Tool in Addressing Serious and Organized Crime', 7-9 December in 4th the Regional Seminar on Good Governance for Southeast Asian Countries, Manila, Philippines, p. 3.
11. 18 U.S. Code § 3771—Crime victims' rights, Retrieved 13 July 2022. https://www.law.cornell.edu/uscode/text/18/3771.
12. The Constitution of Nepal, Article 21.
13. Children Act, 2018, Section 25.
14. Domestic Violence (Crime and Punishment) Act, 2066 (2009), Section 6.
15. Ibid., Section 7.
16. Motor Vehicle and Transportation Management Act, 1993 Sections 160, 161, 163.
17. Criminal Offence (Determination and Execution of Sentence) Act, 2017, Section 13(c).
18. Crime Victim Protection Act, 2019, Section 10.
19. Ibid., Section 4.
20. Ibid., Section 5.
21. Ibid., Section 6.
22. Ibid., Section 11.
23. Ibid.
24. Ibid., Section 13.
25. Ibid., Section 17.
26. Ibid., Section 18.
27. Ibid., Section 19.
28. Ibid., Section 14.
29. Ibid., Section 15.
30. Ibid., Section 12.
31. Suntali Dhami (Shah) *vs.* Office of the Prime Minister and Council of Ministers et al., NKP 2068, vol. 1, Decision No. 8541.

32. NKP 2074 vol. 1, Decision No. 9741.
33. NKP 2067 vol. 11, Decision No. 8507.
34. NKP 2070 vol. 1, Decision No. 8949.
35. NKP 2070 vol. 3, Decision No. 8973.
36. NKP 2064 vol. 9, Decision No. 7880.
37. Supreme Court, Subjectwise Collection of the Summary of Precedent, Criminal Law, Part 2, 2066, p. 1.
38. NKP 2062 vol. 11, Decision No. 7626.
39. NKP 2064 vol. 1, Decision No. 7810.
40. NKP 2072 No. 2, Decision No. 9346.

REFERENCES

Askari, H. (1988). Victimology. *Lex Et Juris, International Current*, 30 July.

Bastola, G.K. (2046 BS). Pidit Kshatipurak Shastra: Ek Charcha (A Discussion on Victimology). Jodhpur: *Kanoon Prakashak*, 11.

Cho, K.S. (2014). The Current Situation and Challenges of Measures for Victims of Crime in the Korean Criminal Justice System. In *The 144th International Senior Seminar Visiting Experts' Papers* (Series 81, p. 77).

Co, M.G. The Enhancement of Appropriate Measures for Victim of Crime at Each Stage of the Philippine Criminal Justice. Retrieved from www.unafei.or.jp/english/pdf/RS_No81/No81_15PA_Co.pdf

Doak, J. (2015). Enriching Trial Justice for Crime Victims in Common Law Systems: Lessons from Transitional Environments. Retrieved from http://irep.ntu.ac.uk/id/eprint/27097/1/PubSub4489_Doak.pdf

Dussich, J.P.J. (2006). Victimology—Past, Present and Future. In *131st International Senior Seminar Visiting Experts' Papers*. Retrieved fromhttps://www.unafei.or.jp/publications/pdf/RS_No70/No70_12VE_ Dussich.pdf

European Union Agency for Fundamental Rights (2019). Justice for victims of violent crime: Part 1 – standards. Retrieved from https://fra.europa.eu/sites/default/files/fra_uploads/fra-2019-justice-for-victims-of-violent-crime-part-1-standards_en.pdf

Jaishankar, K. (2014). Implementing Victims' Rights in Newly-Industrialized Countries: Reflections on Major Challenges and Recommendations for the Future. In *Justice for Victims*.

Kramer, K. (2010). Witness Protection as a Key Tool in Addressing Serious and Organized Crime.

Lindgren, M. and Nikoliæ-Ristanoviæ, V. (2011). *Crime Victims: International and Serbian Perspective.* Organization for Security and Cooperation in Europe, Mission to Serbia, Law Enforcement Department.

Nepal (2011). *Caste-based Discrimination and Untouchability (Offence and Punishment) Act.*

Nepal (2017). *The Country (Muluki) Criminal Code.*

Nepal (2017). *The Country (Muluki) Criminal Procedure Code.*

Nepal (2018). *The Crime Victim Protection Act.*

Nepal (2017). *Criminal Offence (Sentencing and Execution) Act.*

Nepal (2009). *Domestic Violence (Offence and Punishment) Act.*

Nepal (2007). *Human Trafficking and Transportation Control Act.*

Nepal (1993). *Motor Vehicles and Transport Management Act.*

Paulina, V.G. and Carla, F. (2009). Ending Threats and Reprisals Against Victims of Torture and Related International Crimes: A Call to Action. London: The REDRESS Trust.

Romani, C.F. de C. (2010). *International Law of Victims.* Max Planck.

Siddiqu, A.E. (1993). *Criminology Problems and Perspectives.*

Shrestha, S.K. (2001). *A Step Towards Victim Justice System: Nepalese Perspectives* (1st edn.).

——, (2017). *Victimology* (1st edn.). Pairavi Publication.

Tiwari, P. (2012). Victimology: A Sub-Discipline of Criminology. *Dehradun Law Review, 4*(1).

United Nations Office on Drugs and Crime (2009). *Handbook for Professionals and Policymakers on Justice Matters Involving Child Victims and Witnesses of Crime.* Criminal Justice Handbook Series, 1.

United Nations Economic and Social Council (2005). Basic principles on the use of restorative justice programmes in criminal matters. Retrieved from https://www.un.org/en/ecosoc/docs/2005/resolution%202005-20.pdf

United Nations Office on Drugs and Crime (2005). Bangkok declaration: Synergies and responses: Strategic alliances in crime prevention and criminal justice. Retrieved from https://www.unodc.org/pdf/crime/congress11/BangkokDeclaration.pdf

U.S. Code § 3771. Crime victims' rights. Retrieved 13 July 2022, from https://www.law.cornell.edu/uscode/text/18/3771

von Hentig, H. (1940). Remarks on the Interaction of Perpetrator and Victim. *Journal of Criminal Law and Criminology.*

Wemmers, J.A. (2009). Where do they belong? Giving Victims a Place in the Criminal Justice Process. *Criminal Law Forum, 20,* 395. https://doi.org/10.1007/s10609-009-9107-z.

CHAPTER 4

Foundations for Durability and Stability in Democratic Constitutions

REWATI RAJ TRIPATHI AND
PRABHAT CHHETRI

MARXIST APPROACH ON CONSTITUTION AND LAW

Marx distinguished between the economic structure of society (the 'base' or 'infrastructure') and the 'superstructure' which rose upon this 'real foundation'.[1] The term 'superstructure' is used in three senses: (i) legal and political forms which express existing real relations of production; (ii) forms of consciousness which express a particular class view of the world; and (iii) a process in which individuals become aware of fundamental economic conflicts and fight those out.[2]

Examining the relationship between Capitalism and Marxism concerning law and constitutional interpretation reveals significant divergence in their perspectives. Marxist ideology interprets law through three fundamental principles: dialectical materialism, the law of production and historical materialism. In contrast, capitalists view the constitution and law as inherently self-sustaining entities, treating concepts like the rule of law, capitalist or bourgeois societal structures and the separation of powers as immutable truths.

Nevertheless, Marxists view law as a tool wielded by the ruling class to oppress the governed. In a class-based society, law serves as a weapon used by the dominant class to subjugate the subordinate class. It does not exist in isolation but functions as a superstructure built upon the economic and social foundations of society, shaped by economic forces. For Marx, while philosophers have interpreted the world, the ultimate duty lies over turning it for a better one. Thus, involving society and understanding law as dynamic are essential corner stones for a successful legal system.

According to Marxist theory, all ideological constructs, including religion, moral philosophy, art, as well as political and legal institutions, are not autonomous entities but rather grounded in the economic and political framework of society. These constructs do not derive from any inherent or eternal notions of law and justice. In Marxist thought, law and the state are inseparable; a state devoid of law is inconceivable. In the earliest stages of societal formation, such as in primitive communist societies, there was an absence of formal legal systems, a characteristic that is anticipated to persist in future communist societies. With the emergence of the concept of personal property, societal classes began to form, leading to the progression through various socioeconomic stages—including slave societies, feudal societies, capitalist societies and socialist societies—all culminating in the eventual establishment of a communist society. In this future communist society, economic contradictions are expected to be resolved, thereby ending the exploitation of individuals by others and rendering the law, as a tool of exploitation, unnecessary.

During the transitional phase from capitalism to socialism and ultimately to communism, following a proletarian-led revolution, the role of law persists as a mechanism for facilitating the transition. Throughout this transitional period, the law serves multiple functions, including the facilitation of the collective ownership of means of production, in doctrination of individuals in communist ideals and the suppression of reactionary movements seeking to revert to previous socioeconomic structures. Therefore, during this transition, the law is viewed as a two-edged tool that is employed to educate the public and quell counterrevolutionary elements. However, as society moves closer to communism, the need for laws as tools of oppression decreases, eventually causing them to become outdated and wither away.

The following three laws of materialist dialectic are: the law of unity and struggle of opposites, law of quantitative to qualitative change and law of negation of negation. The unity and struggle between opposites constitute the fundamental law of materialist dialectic. According to this principle, every object embodies two conflicting aspects, which engage in perpetual conflict, compelled to intermingle for their own sustenance. Both aspects are dynamic and vibrant, often transforming into each other under certain circumstances. For instance, capitalists and the proletariat represent mutually contradictory facets of society. While their interests diverge, they are intricately intertwined internally, forming a unity between opposing elements. The capitalists have to buy labour power for production and the workers have to sell labour power to satisfy their needs, indicating a unity between opposite forces. However, class struggle between them is still fierce as capitalists try to make as much profit as possible while workers want to ensure higher wages. This central conflict clearly shows that these two concepts are often at odds with each other.

When conflicting forces struggle for dominance, a victor may emerge, or a new element may develop, signifiying a change. These changes can be categorized into two types: quantitative and qualitative.

A gradual progression within an object without altering its form or quality constitutes a quantitative change. Conversely, a qualitative change involves a radical transformation in both form and quality, often occurring suddenly. For example, the gradual heating of water illustrates a quantitative change as the water retains its form and properties throughout the process. However, once the temperature reaches 100° Celsius, the water undergoes a qualitative change, boiling and transforming into steam and exhibiting distinct properties and form.

The third principle, the law of the negation of negation, refers to the replacement of one entity by another. While this process may seem to replicate the original entity, it ultimately leads to the emergence of a qualitatively distinct object. This principle applies to societal development as well. The emergence of class society negated primitive communist societies, while future communist societies will negate class societies. Similarly, the evolution from spontaneous materialism to mechanical materialism and subsequently to dialectical materialism, exemplifies the negation of negation. However, in the envisioned classless society of the future, where conflicting classes are absent, this process of negation will cease. It is believed that in such a society, where economic and social structures will be separated, exploitation and class differentiation will disappear, eliminating both rulers and the ruled, as well as exploiters and the exploited.

CONSTITUTION AS A POLITICO-LEGAL DOCUMENT

Advocates of capitalist democracy regard the law as relatively autonomous but they consider the constitution as a politico-legal document. The constitution encompasses principles and practices that establish the fundamental framework of governance for an organized political community. It directs politics by defining the distribution and utilization of state power. The constitution is both a political and a legal document, as it ensures the freedoms and rights of citizens, legally regulates the government and can be enforced by the courts.

Marxists or socialists perceive the constitution crafted under their leadership as a revolutionary manifesto. Constitutions emerging after socialist revolutions aim to comprehensively overhaul established civil societies based on the principles and achievements of the original social revolution, reflecting the ideologies and impacts inherent in it. Such constitutions are designed to dismantle existing structures entirely and redefine their components. They delineate the rights, roles and responsibilities within the state system, excluding political participation from specific classes (counter-revolutionary classes). In such contexts, ultimate authority over the state resides in the hands of well-organized revolutionary leaders.[3]

In contrast, when a state system arises from compromise, the constitution is typically formulated through collaboration among stakeholders or a conference of stakeholders. State power is distributed among various entities through the participation of stakeholders under the principles of federalism. In class-based political systems, where two distinct classes coexist, one class views itself as the sole architect of the nation's fate, assuming the privilege and responsibility of drafting the constitution, which is subsequently conferred by the higher authorities. The role of the other class primarily involves adhering to the provisions of the constitution, where consent is characterized by faith or allegiance to authority. Examples of top-down constitutions given by ruling classes include those proclaimed by monarchs during the medieval period and constitutions prior to the Second People's Movement.

FOUNDATIONS OF DURABILITY AND STABILITY OF THE CONSTITUTION

Advocates of capitalist democracy consider the constitution as a sacred document based on democratic constitutionalism and generally do not accept its rewriting. It is due to the circumstances surrounding the capitalist revolution, which recently liberated itself from British imperialism. Thomas Jefferson, one of the architects of the American Constitution, remarked to James Madison in discussion that the Constitution should be rewritten by every generation,[4] emphasizing that the deceased should not dictate governance to the living. The US Constitution of 1789 stands as the oldest surviving constitution. Historian Steven Ming writes that the United States has the oldest written national framework of government in the world.[5] By the end of the twentieth century, he writes, 159 countries had written constitutions and 101 of those had been in practice since 1970.[6] However, America is the only nation that has been governed by the same constitution for two centuries.

On the other hand, in France, around the same time—namely, after the French Revolution in 1789—fifteen constitutions were enacted following the Constitution of the First Republic, issued in 1791. Consequently, among the contemporaneous constitutions, the American constitution has endured for approximately 230 years with only twenty-seven amendments. Through this constitution, the nation, recently liberated from imperialism, was able to evolve into the world's most powerful country, despite enduring two civil wars and two world wars. On the other hand, France enacted 16 constitutions during the same period of upheaval and considering the average lifespan of these constitutions, it appears that a new constitution was drafted approximately every twenty years. More surprisingly, the French Additional Act of 1815 was enforced for only twenty-one days.

Before discussing the reasons for this, it is relevant to discuss the background of the constitution. The constitution lays down the basic principles governing the state's operation. As a framework of government, the constitution describes the basic structure of the government, institutions and political process. Additionally, as a protector of rights, it declares certain rights as fundamental or basic rights and outlines measures for their protection within society. Constitutions designed post-revolution or after reform movements incorporate agendas raised during the revolution and the aim to address the people's expectations during the implementation of the constitution. The success of a constitution is largely determined by its ability to meet the expectations placed upon it.

The durability of the Constitution is not an end in itself. Jefferson contends that the Constitution serves as a remedial measure. Professor Joshua Saylor of Sandra Day O'Connor College of Law argues that the framers of the American Constitution aimed to foster democratic discourse, safeguard against governmental fragmentation and abuse and equitably distribute power among the three branches of government. Post-revolution, they established a government independent from the legislature to embody the desire for a sufficiently robust central authority, thus ensuring the Constitution's durability. Some scholars attribute the enduring nature of the US Constitution to the wisdom of its framers, who crafted a document featuring a separation and balance of powers, concise language and a judicial activism. Particularly, the judiciary's role in interpreting the Constitution according to contemporary needs has facilitated its adaptation without formal amendments. The trust and reliance of citizens and other governmental branches on the judiciary play a pivotal role in upholding the longevity of the US Constitution. Martin H. Redish distinguishes the American Constitution as a consensual social agreement, contrasting it with the French Constitution, which is viewed as a subject of contention. As a result, the American Constitution endured, whereas the French Constitution has been subject to frequent changes.

Even in our context, the people's expectations at the time of drafting the constitution played a pivotal role. Since the people's movement in 2007 BS was aimed to transfer the authority from the Rana to the King, the public was not particularly focused about the constitution. Indeed, in the royal declaration made by King Tribhuvan on 7 Falgun 2007 BS he proclaimed that '. . . today it is our wish and decision that the government of our people should be in accordance with the republican constitution drafted by a Constituency Assembly elected by them. . .'. However, when King Mahendra came to power, he adopted the policy of dividing and ruling the political parties. Until the year 2015 BS, there was no constitution, no elections and the breakdown of democratic power, as the King manipulated the political parties. However, the political leadership at that time believed that everything could be put back on track after the enactment of a parliamentary constitution and the election of the government.

Unfortunately, the elected government did not gain momentum after the King took power. Consequently, the political parties had to struggle for the restoration of the parliamentary system for three decades.

In bourgeois democracy, there is a strong emphasis on political and civil rights and freedoms. This principle was evident in the 2046 BS people's movement, where both local and foreign bourgeois democratic forces shared the common goal of leading the movement and ensuring it remained free from the influence of leftist ideologies. As a result, the people's movement was characterized with limited political freedom.

After the 2046 BS people's movement, the primary ally of the movement, the Samyukta Janamorcha, not only faced complete disregard but was also prohibited. About the constitution, which initially prioritized political and civil freedoms, along with the poor governance of elected government, the Chairman of the Maoists' affiliate organization, Samyukta Janamorcha, Baburam Bhattarai, handed over a 40-point petition to then Prime Minister Sher Bahadur Deuba. The petition outlined various points, including the abolition of unequal treaties such as the Nepal-India Treaty of 1950 (Point No. 1); ending the dominance of monopoly capital in Nepal's economy and establishing customs policies to foster a self-sufficient national economy (Point Nos. 6 and 7); drafting a new constitution by elected representatives to establish democracy and end royal privileges (Point Nos. 10 and 11); declaring Nepal a secular state (Point No. 18); ensuring equal rights for daughters to ancestral property (Point No. 19); ending all forms of caste-based exploitation and oppression and establishing ethnicity-based self-governance in areas where a particular ethnic community constitutes a majority (Point No. 20); eradicating discrimination against Dalits should be and completely abolishing the practice of untouchability (Point No. 21); providing equal opportunities and facilities for all language speakers, with arrangements for education in the mother tongue up to the higher secondary level (Point No. 22); strengthening and empowering local bodies (Point No. 26); and providing free and scientific health and education services for all (Point No. 35).[7] The neglect of these demands by the government led to a decade-long civil war, known as the People's War, which ultimately brought an end to the 240-year-old feudal monarchy and paved the way for a federal, republican, inclusive and secular state, leading to the drafting of a new constitution.

Although the Nepali Civil War concluded through an agreement prompted by national and international circumstances, numerous political agendas highlighted the conflict, along with certain economic, social and cultural rights, enshrined as fundamental rights in the constitution. A constitution created in the aftermath of a revolution must reflect the spirit of the movement and lay the groundwork for fulfilling its expectations. Mere words within the constitution cannot automatically meet the people's aspirations; it is the state's institutions and their actors that must bring them to life. The most crucial aspect is building trust among citizens that the constitution and its associated institutions are addressing their expectations. Achieving this, fosters hope among the public, although this alone does not guarantee the longevity of the constitution.

PEOPLE-ORIENTED PROVISIONS UNDER THE NEPALI PREVAILING CONSTITUTION

Nepal underwent seven decades of both large- and small-scale armed conflicts, as well as peaceful protests and demonstrations, to achieve a comprehensive democratic constitution. Following the 2062-3 BS movement, when the Constituent Assembly enacted the new constitution in 2072 BS, it was declared that the era of political struggle had ended and the focus shifted to economic revolution. This indicated that all major political issues had been addressed through the constitution. In essence, the nation transitioned into a secular, federal and inclusive republic, where individuals from all walks of life can aspire to the highest positions in the country. The introduction of federalism has paved the way for equitable development, while the assurance of economic and social rights signifies that further political upheaval is unnecessary.

The current constitution, drafted by the Constituent Assembly, emphasizes its commitment to socialism directly in its preamble. It seeks to eradicate all forms of discrimination and oppression departing from the feudal, despotic, centralized and unitary state system, thereby ensuring social justice. Article 3 of the Constitution defines the nation with multi-ethnic, multilingual, multi-religious, multicultural characteristics, while Article 4 characterizes the state as a secular, inclusive, socialism-oriented and federal democratic republican. These foundational principles hold immense significance and pose a challenge to feudal powers.

In addition to these core provisions, the fundamental right enshrined in Part Three of the constitution—especially the newly introduced rights—highlight the socialist and inclusive character of the constitution. Article 16 affirms that every person has the right to live with dignity, implying that Nepali citizens are entitled to lead a dignified life, secured by basic rights and their effective enforcement. The responsibility of ensuring this lies with the state. Similarly, Article 24 of the Constitution guarantees the right against untouchability and discrimination as a fundamental right. This article stipulates that no person shall be subjected to any form of untouchability or discrimination in any private or public places on grounds of his or her origin, caste, tribe, community, profession, occupation or physical condition. Additionally, there should be no discrimination in the production or distribution of goods, services or facilities. It is universally recognized as a fundamental human right that individuals should not face discrimination based on factors such as gender, ethnic origin, colour, political beliefs, religious affiliations or sexual orientation.

Likewise, Article 32 provides for the right to language and culture, Article 33 guarantees the right to employment, Article 34 enshrines the right to labour, Article 35 ensures the right to health, Article 36 establishes the right to food sovereignty, Article 37 secures the right to shelter and Article 38 safeguards the rights of women. These rights represent the collective entitlements of the people. It seems that many of the demands outlined in the petition presented by the Samyukta Janamorcha prior to the enactment of the constitution have been incorporated into it.

Article 42 of the constitution outlines the right to social justice, ensuring the inclusion of socially backward classes, including women, in state bodies based on inclusive principles. Additionally, Article 42(2) mandates that indigent citizens and citizens and communities on the verge of extinction shall have the right to get special opportunities and benefits in education, health, housing, employment, food and social security for their protection, uplift-ment, empowerment and development.

Moreover, the guiding principles of the state in Part Four of the Constitution also reflects its socialist orientation. Due to space constraints, a detailed discussion of these principles is not feasible here.

EXAMINING CONSTITUTIONAL DURABILITY AND STABILITY: KEY INQUIRIES

Concerns about the Constitution's durability and stability have occasionally arisen in the seven years following its enactment. While dissatisfaction was widespread at the time of its adoption, the intensity of criticism has since diminished. Initially, certain political factions denounced the constitution as flawed, but with time, many of these groups have come to accept it in practice. In addition to participating in electoral processes under the constitution, these factions have also engaged in government formation, thereby tacitly acknowledging its provisions. What began as demands for a complete rewrite of the constitution has gradually transitioned into calls for constitutional amendments. This shift signifies a growing acceptance and adoption of the constitution. It is essential to view such demands for amendment positively, recognizing that no constitution can be immutable. To ensure its relevance and efficacy, periodic amendments and developments through formal procedures, judicial interpretations and practical applications are imperative.

In recent times, concerns regarding the stability of the constitution have emerged. These concerns do not reflect the rejection of the constitution itself but rather echoes the concern over the individuals entrusted with the responsibility of governing the state within its framework and those who have taken solemn oaths to safeguard its integrity. Notably, frequent dissolution of the House of Representatives through mechanisms not sanctioned by the constitution, reluctance to form a government despite enjoying majority support from parliamentarians and reluctance to endorse bills passed by both houses, particularly when additional questions not included in the original text of bill are raised, have reignited doubts about the constitution's stability.

The first condition for the constitution to endure is for everyone to embrace its provisions, which entails internal acceptance. In practice, the effectiveness of the constitution is demonstrated by the exercise of rights and adherence to duties outlined within it. Distinguished jurist H.L.A. Hart suggests that for a constitution or any law to be effective, it must achieve a minimum level of effectiveness, especially in a developed society where it should be embraced and adhered to by state officials as a rule governing their formal conduct. This is also referred to as constitutional culture, which entails understanding and interpreting the constitution's provisions. Unfortunately, we have yet to cultivate a strong constitutional culture. There is a tendency to interpret the constitution's provisions subjectively, which poses challenges to its implementation and sustainability. This factor also contributed to the failure of the 2047 BS constitution.

It can be observed that even political factions which initially expressed extreme dissatisfaction when the constitution was promulgated, have subsequently participated in elections conducted in accordance with its provisions and have agreed to amend the constitution without revising it entirely. This suggests that discontent at the civil level is gradually dissipating. However, in such a scenario, it is gravely concerning that the responsible stakeholders of the state, who are entrusted with the guardianship of the constitution, has exceeded its constitutional limits. Given that the constitution itself grants the Supreme Court the authority to determine the constitutionality of bills and invalidate them if found to be unconstitutional, attempts made to nullify this right to interpret the constitution will be questioned for a long time.

The second vital aspect for ensuring the longevity of the constitution is fostering a sense of ownership among the populace. It is imperative for everyone to feel connected to the constitution. This sense of ownership can be nurtured through active participation in its creation and by addressing grievances through amendments. To ensure the widespread acceptance of the constitution, it is crucial to promptly address emerging issues since its promulgation. This serves as a safety mechanism for the constitution. The 2047 constitution retained certain provisions as basic principles while allowing for amendments on other matters. However, the failure to utilize this safety mechanism to address immediate grievances through amendments led to the downfall of the constitution. During discussions about amending the constitution, there were objections from the establishment side against altering trivial matters. Nonetheless, the constitution was repealed without any attempt at amendment.

The development of the constitution takes place through its application, court interpretation and through formal amendments. The things that are not in the constitution or the provisions that are not clear can be developed through good practice, which can also be referred to as organic development. To alleviate dissatisfaction with the current constitution, an acceptable amendment draft can be prepared through thorough discussion and consultation, addressing concerns through constitutional amendment. This could be a significant step toward ensuring the stability of the constitution.

In our context, the third thing necessary for the stability of the constitution is the actual projection of rights. Although the constitution has adopted a federal model, the trend of centralization of rights has not improved. It is necessary for everyone to understand that all three levels of government are under the rule of the constitution and are independent in their areas and should function accordingly. Our political leadership has not internalized the function of provincial government and local bodies as that of government.

The fourth condition for the longevity constitution is the democratization of institutions. Democracy demands participation, discussion and transparency in policymaking. The more the state institutions are democratic, the people's trust in democracy increases. This helps in the longevity of the democratic constitution.

The fifth important condition is good governance and development. People want to improve their standard of living. Moreover, democracy is for advanced and prosperous life. The constitution is not an end but a means to achieve a high and prosperous life through the democratic process. No matter how good the constitution is, if prosperity is not achieved, the people will not be satisfied. Therefore, we should be able to make the people optimistic that this constitution is ours, the government is for us and the government works for our welfare.

The sixth condition is the actual participation of the people. The current elections are only formal and syndicate based. Elections are expensive. There have been instances where some good politicians have hesitated to contest the election. It is necessary to improve the electoral system and make it less expensive. As a result, people's participation will increase, people's democracy will be established and the people themselves will protect and own the democratic constitution.

The seventh condition is the democratization of political parties. Political parties are the cornerstone of democracy. Apparently, there is lack of internal democracy in political parties. The political parties operate with a bureaucratic approach that is subject to the whims of certain leaders. To increase people's faith in democracy, parties themselves should adopt democratic practices. Enhanced internal democratic practices strengthen democracy, foster the growth of democratic culture and consequently heighten public appeal.

The eighth thing is to develop a sense of responsibility. Democracy is a system of public accountability. If the people feel that the representatives sent by them are sensitive and responsible towards them, they will believe in political parties, democracy and the constitution.

The ninth thing is to implement the inclusiveness adopted by the constitution in practice. At present, inclusivity is not given attention in state agencies, political parties or election candidates. The people's faith in the constitution cannot be maintained when the expectations that led to participation in the democratic movement are not fulfilled.

The tenth and last condition is the practical implementation of various economic, social and cultural rights guaranteed by the constitution. The practical implementation of important economic, social and cultural rights such as the right to live in a clean environment, the right to education, the right to language and religion, the right to food, the right to housing, the right to social security, the right to health and the right to consumers is essential for the perpetuation of the constitution.

However, the situation is different in the twentieth century. Constitutions enacted after the revolutions largely resembles the revolutionary manifestos, often structured upon the ideals and accomplishments of original social revolutions, aiming to comprehensively reshape established civil societies. These therefore aim at completely dismantling previous structures and redefining them with a view of integrating previously excluded groups into the country's governance. Even though they are considered as instruments of change, sometimes they show a society-state connection that is far from reality hence calling for reforms whenever there is a wide difference between fiction and truth. As such, amendments or changes have been sought to build a new political order through constitutionality. However, if the power structure of the state cannot be fully reshaped then it becomes difficult to implement such constitutions practically. The effective implementation of constitutional provisions necessitates cooperation from all institutions within the state structure, including the courts, military, police and other constitutional and administrative bodies. Without such cooperation, the realization of constitutional provisions becomes unattainable. Currently, we are experiencing a similar situation.

CONCLUSION

In conclusion, the constitution stands as the cornerstone of the political landscape, which is rightly recognized as a political-legal document. Our prevailing constitution reflects a compromise between established and emerging powers, akin to a contractual agreement where rights and responsibilities are distributed among all stakeholders. Upholding the longevity of our democratic constitution requires firm commitment from all the stakeholders to adhere to its principles. This emphasizes the importance of fostering a democratic culture among political actors, guiding their actions to align with constitutional provisions. Furthermore, embracing judicial interpretations is crucial for ensuring the resilience of our democratic system in the long run.

NOTES

1. Freeman, M.D.A. (2021). *Lloyd's Introduction to Jurisprudence.* London, Sweet and Maxwell, Reprinted in India, p. 958.
2. Ibid.
3. Daniel J. Elazar (1990). Constitution-Making: The Pre-eminently Political Act, Constitutionalism: The Israeli and American Experiences, JCPA, https://www.jcpa.org/dje/articles3/constisramer.htm.
4. Tom Ginsburg et al. (2009). 'The Endurance of National Constitutions', Cambridge University Press, p. 1.

5. Ibid.
6. Steven Mintz, '*Historical Context: The Survival of the US Constitution*', https://www.gilderlehrman.org/history-resources/teaching-resource/historical-context-survival-us-constitution
7. Baburam's demand to Baburam himself, Retrieved from https://mysansar.com/2012/06/506/

REFERENCES

Bhattarai, Baburam (2012). Baburam's demand to Baburam himself. Retrieved from https://mysansar.com/2012/06/506/

Elazar, D.J. (1990). Constitution-making: The Pre-eEinentlyPolitical Act. In *Constitutionalism: The Israeli and American Experiences.* Retrieved from https://www.jcpa.org/dje/articles3/constisramer.htm

Freeman, M.D.A. (2021). *Lloyd's Introduction to Jurisprudence.* London: Sweet and Maxwell.

Ginsburg, T., Elkins, Z., and Melton, J. (2009). *The Endurance of National Constitutions.* Cambridge: Cambridge University Press.

Mintz, S. (n.d.). *Historical Context: The Survival of the US Constitution.* Retrieved from https://www.gilderlehrman.org/history-resources/teaching-resource/historical-context-survival-us-constitution.

CHAPTER 5

Fragmented Unions: The Social Facets of Living Together in Contemporary Capitalist Societies

NARAYANI DEVKOTA

INTRODUTION

In sociology, marriage is one of the many important social institutions alongside religious, educational, political, economic and employment-related institutions. In the normative (conventional) definition marriage is a permanent (lifelong) relationship between male and female for permanent sexual relation, reproduction of human life and sharing all matters of their lives. Along with this, marriage is also considered a socio-cultural right and responsibility. These rights and responsibilities are not only towards their partner but also towards their in-laws. In common terms, marriage is a relationship between two opposite sexes, who are young by their age, sexually virgin as well as also monogamous. In this regard heterosexual marriage is often analysed as an 'oppressive institution' toward women from view point of Marxist and feminist perspective. Sexual relationship before marriage, without marital status and in widowhood was restricted specially toward women in Hindu religious society. It manifested in practices like the 'Sati'[1] system and widowhood[2] which reflect without colour red of Hindu religion and the wearing of white dress in a wedding occasion in Christianity.[3] Giving birth without wedding is legally restricted in various countries.[4]

In one sentence, marriage is both social and legal foundation to fulfil a person's sexual and reproductive desire, to live together, to share and collective earning, sharing and owning of their property and mutual right and responsibility towards their partner and in-laws. Philosophical developments offer a logical understanding of the phenomena, while science and technology provide support. The capitalist mode of production has scattered individuals from familiar societies to unknown ones, leading to alienation. With these changes in social conceptions normative definition of marriage has also changed. With the growth of science and technology the forms of purity and pollution of sexuality started to be criticized and became less restricted. At present, we can see various rupture in marriage as social institution. We can see these ruptures in various aspects of society, i.e. people prefer living together (co-habitation) and many people fall in love with those people who belong from the same sex. It is also seen that many people live without marriage, without any partner and many women became mothers out of wedlock. Divorce and remarriage or late-age marriage has become common all over the world.

Marriage as social institution we can analyse through various sociological theories, such as Marxism, Feminism, Structural Functionality and Modernism. From the Marxist point of view marriage is an oppressive institution toward women and children so we need to abolish it. Feminism also has nearly the same thought that it's oppressive through the various ways toward women. But structural functionalist perspective focuses on social cohesion and social integrity which support to maintain social order and run society functionally by marriage too. So social institution became important from the viewpoint of structural functionalism. Theories of modernism, which provide the aspect of rational thought, behave and function became modern in society with the changing social structure. Modernism specially can be seen on *Gemeinschalf and Gesellschaft* of Ferdinand Tönnies (1957). Mechanical solidarity and organic solidarity are a part of Emile Durkheim's theory of the development of societies in, *The Division of Labour in Society* (1893).

In this article, I will provide a concise theoretical exploration of matrimony and examine the global dynamics of living together (cohabitation), with a special focus on the context within Nepal.

MARXIST CRITICISM TO MARRIAGE AND FAMILY

At the dawn of the Marxist philosophy, with the declaration of communist movement through *The Communist Manifesto* in 1848, Marx and Engels declare their position on the modern bourgeois family relation as oppressive toward women and will eventually disappear with the capitalist mode of production. Marx and Engels wrote:

> Abolition of the family! Even the most radical flare up at this infamous proposal of the communists.
>
> On what foundation is the present family, the bourgeois family based? On capital, on private gain. In its completely developed form, this family exists only among the bourgeoisie. But this state of things finds its complement in the practical absence of the family among the proletarians and in public prostitution. The bourgeois family will vanish as a matter of course when its complement vanishes and both will vanish with the vanishing of capital. (Marx and Engels, 1848).

After the declaration of *The Communist Manifesto* Engels published his groundbreaking book *Family, Private Property, and Origins of State* in 1884 based on Morgan's work and Marx's notes. The book reached a wider audience and advocated the abolition of family structure.

However, now in the European continent there is the debate that living together (cohabitation) relation rose after the demolition of Soviet Union. Arland Thornton and Dimiter Philipov write in their article:

> In central and Eastern Europe, during the late 1980s and early 1990s, there were major political changes, such as the fall of communist governments. These societies entered a new era of increased social freedom, less rigid rules and less authoritarian governments. They interacted with western Europe and some become members of the European Union. As a result, the pattern of family

life has changed, marriage rates have declined and marriage was postponed to a later age. Cohabitation and births to unmarried mothers increased and in some countries the increase was very quick (Thornton and Philipov, 2009).

It shows that the communism does not force to abolish the marriage relationship.

MODERNISM ON MARRIAGE AND FAMILY

Modernity theory suggests that scientific advancement has diminished religious influence on individuals, particularly regarding sexuality. Living with emotional or physical attachment was stigmatized in Christian society too. But Pope Francis started to give marital status for those people who were in live-in relationship. According to the news published on 15 September 2014 at Australian Broadcasting Corporation (ABC), 'Pope Francis break taboo by marrying cohabiting couples, conducts mass wedding ceremony.' Liberal political thought also provides the ground to develop personal relationship as love partner, sex partner or other relationship.

FEMINIST CRITIQUE ON MARRIAGE AND FAMILY

Like Marxists, feminists also criticize the concept of marriage. From the feminist corner, marriage controls the women's dignity economically, socio-culturally, symbolically and on their identity by and under patriarchal norms, values, power and politics. It is not only in one society, nearly all over the world.

Socio-culturally, white wedding dress of Christianity is depicted as the virginity of women and non-virgin girl negatively. And also, Christianity did not allow the sexual desire of women. Clare Chambers (2013) write on her article 'The Marriage Free State':

> The white wedding is replete with sexist imagery the father 'giving away' the bride; the white dress symbolizing the bride's virginity and emphasizing the importance of her appearance; the vows to obey the husband; the minister telling the husband 'you may now kiss the bride' (rather than the

bride herself giving permission, on indeed initiating or at least equally participating in the act of kissing); the reception at which, traditionally, all the speeches are given by men; the wife surrendering her own name and taking her husband's.

Socio-cultural norms in Nepal, once manifested in the Sati and Widow practices, now continue through early teen *Gunyu Choli* and *Kanyadan* during marriage. Despite the legal abolition of Sati, these enduring customs still shape women's dignity and autonomy.

Economically, marriage provides the ground for gendered division of labour, which is unpaid care work and counted as non-productive work. Talking about feminists, the groundbreaking work of Betty Friedan's *The Feminine Mystique* (1963) gives the new way of thought of marriage as the unsolved problem of materially prosperous housewife of America. She starts this book with the description she called 'the problem that has no name'. This unnamed problem widely spread unhappiness of women in the 1950s and 1960s America and after 1990s in Nepal. Married women were unhappy despite good living condition and having a child too. On her book Friedan also questions the women's magazine, women's education system and advertisers for creating this widespread image of women. The harmful effects induced by this image were that it cornered women into the domestic sphere and it led many women to lose their own identity.

We can see a similar criticism in Nepali Feminist movement after 1990s political change and they have advocated the count of women's domestic work. The publication of *Status of Women in Nepal: Statistical Profile of Nepalese Women* (1979), gives a logical understanding of unpaid domestic work also as work. Government of Nepal is still unable to incorporate how to recognize domestic work on system. But it creates great social understanding which provide the knowledge to develop women's liberation and individual's freedom.

RISE OF LIVING TOGETHER

Living together is a relationship between two individual living as a couple without socio-cultural and legal recognition and they don't have socio-cultural as well as a legal right and responsibility too. They share everything such as household responsibility, economic condition, sexual desire and pleasure without socio-cultural and legal recognition. There are various words as synonyms of 'living together'[5] but in this article all these terminologies are used as only 'living together'.

Living together is an alternative or modern form of conventional marriage institution. There is diverse analysis on the debate that 'living together' is new phenomenon or old phenomenon. Some writers wrote that it's a new phenomenon (Scott, 2008), (Chambers, 2013), (Thornton and Philipov, 2009), (Kien, 2018) and Anastasia de Waal who is a head of the Education and family Unit of Civitas, a UK-based think tank wrote in his article *Cohabitation* that 'Cohabitation, when a couple live together in a sexual partnership without being married, is not a new phenomenon. It is estimated between the mid-eighteenth and mid-nineteenth centuries, either as a precursor to marriage or as an informal alternative.'

But in the same article he writes that cohabitation became progressively more widespread across society toward the second half of the twentieth century, with a significant rise since the mid-1980. So, there can be no contention that living together (cohabitation) was not a new phenomenon, it was prevalent in a scattered way before 1970s too, but it rapidly increased after 1970s. In Nepal too, living together was rising after the political change of 1990s, in the areas of comparatively developed urban areas like Kathmandu, Pokhara, Dharan. But, in Nepal we do not have any authentic data stating how many people are in live-in relationship. The big survey, such as Census, Nepal Demographic Health Survey, Nepal Living Standard Survey of government are still unable to recognize that living together has also been practiced in Nepali society.

In the absence of authentic data, we do not know how many people are in live-in relationship. According to the news published in *Setopati* in 2080,[6] monthly ten to fifteen young girls came to the Women Commission to register complain that 'after living together he did not get married with me'. This data indicates that there are various couple who live under the live-in relationship.

In the public sphere, we engage in the debate concerning the social change and recognition of living together. It was stigmatized as socially unsocial behaviour, cultural sin, and over freedom. Living together is depicted in Nepali news (paper, radio, TV and social media such as Facebook, Twitter, YouTube) comes as a cause of crime, such as killing,[7,8,9] domestic violence,[10] depression and suicide[11], honey trapping, birth of unwanted child and violence[12], leaving a child in garbage, forest and infanticide. Sometimes it is depicted as a bargaining tool to exploit another partner. And from the side of human right activist, 'living together' relationship is also suppressive for women and girls.

Social perception also depends on the level of knowledge, freedom, awareness and social connectivity on how people enjoy with living together. Empirically we can see a prism of live-in relationship and in these multicoloured relationship impact differently in individual's life. Some people are enjoying it as liberation and freedom, while some are waiting for time and situation to get married, some individual are suffering from the burden of unwanted child, some people are suffering from domestic violence and some people lose their life through the killing too, some people are in psychological trauma, threat of life, some children are suffering economically, physically and emotionally through the parent's choice of living together. With the lack of authentic data, we do not know how many people have better peaceful relationship and how many individuals are suffering from it.

However, there are various forms of living together in Nepal such as early age marriage which are socio-culturally recognized but legally not married, heterosexual couple and legally not recognized youth heterosexual couple, socio-culturally not recognized homosexual couple, extramarital relationship holder couple and so on. Living relationship is socially stigmatizing, controversial and sensitive relationship even in highly modern and educated Kathmandu valley.

Nepal police office, courts, media and NGO worker often see a dark side of living together.[13] Rather than the claim of the Marxism, Feminism and Modernism, the public face of living together as the alternative of marriage relation 'as oppressive institution' is vulgar for those people. Along with the killing, depression, suicide, there are various impact on children whose parents are not legally recognized as husband and wife. High rate of illegal abortion, leaving a child in garbage, domestic violence, facing difficulties to get birth certificate, getting government's identity such as citizenship is hard without the marriage registration of parents. Socially they are unable to fully enjoy with their parent's culture and social surrounding, especially with their grandparent, uncle, aunts and cousins and they are also not recognized by these social groups.

Academically we have few research on living together in Nepal. One among this few research is of Bishnu Prasad Dahal's 'Live-in relationship' towards a new pattern of adult life in Kathmandu (2020). His study is based on case studies on Kathmandu District Court after separation of individual from the living together. He wrote that:

> The field study was carried out amongst respondents who go away from living together and those respondents were key respondents who filed the cases in Kathmandu District Court after separation. Most of the cases are filed under the clauses that the female partner was raped by her male partner while they were in live-in relationship.

This research is unable to give the cause of living together rather it gives the glimpses of violence within the live-in relationship.

As authentic data depicts, Government of Nepal also does not have legal background to recognize the live-in relationship and formulation of the separate law on living together. But it is clear from Article 74 of the Civil Code of 2074 that 'if a woman is found to have conceived and given birth to a child through physical contact with a man, such marriage shall be deemed to have occurred automatically'. It's somehow the ground of legal recognition of child and father relationship. But not a solution of forced abortion, negligence, domestic violence against partner (not only a women) and child. This legal recognition is problematic too. Advocate Alpana Bhandari writes on her blog:

> This means that if a child is born while a man and a woman are in physical contact, the law seeks to encompass both the child and the relationship that has been established in this manner. However, it should not be assumed that every child born in this manner is the result of a cohabitation connection. A baby can be born when a woman is sexually abused, when a man and a woman engage in sexual activity to satisfy their sexual desires, or when they engage in romantic activity.

Bhandari and senior advocate Shashi Adhikari have similar thoughts toward the provision of Civil Code of 2074. It's not the legal recognition of living together, and it's unable to solve the problem relating to the living together.

To recognize the live-in relationship, in 2078 two different committee of House of Representatives, i.e. Women and Social Committee and Law, Justice and Human Rights Committee discussed the issue of living together and criminalization of relationship. These two different meetings focused on registration of the relationship as couple under the government's rules and regulation. Similarly, senior advocate Shashi Adhikari, Mohan Acharya have been advocating for legal recognition of live-in relationship. Last time, in first Chaitra 2080, advocate Annu Bhattarai filed a writ petition to Supreme Court urging for the legal status for live-in relationship.[14]

But from the corner of LGBTIQ community, they are focused on same sex marriage, and demanding the marital right as hetero-sexual people. After the rise of Gay liberation movement particularly and LGBTIQ movement generally demanding the marital status indicate that marriage is also a privilege to enjoy the sexual, reproductive and socio-cultural life. And there is a prominent question, which form of marriage is oppressive? Or there is a question 'Marriage is oppressive for whom?'

Clare Chambers, a British political philosopher at the Faculty of Philosophy at the University of Cambridge, writes on her article *The Marriage Free State* which was published on 2013, that there are two types of critics specially from the feminist corner such as marriage as oppressive institution and it is privileges only for those who has hetero sexuality. In Nepal too for some individual, live-in relationship is preferred because they do not have the legal privilege to register their relationship and socio-culturally family and society are unable to accept their relationship.

As Chambers states, also in Nepal marriage is a privilege to those people who are unable to register their relationship and they also suffered from emotional breakdown, multiple relationship and violence. According to Durga Thapa, whose interview is collected in the book named Samanata Ko Rile Daud (2021), where she is one among twelve interviewees. She said that there are various cases of emotional torture, multiple relationship, battering and economic exploitation in the same sex relationship too. Within the women right movement in Nepal, they are together with other women in some part of movement. But same-sex (lesbian) women are now in that position to fight for already established right for women. These already established right is right to get marriage and to establish own family. Thapa (2021) said,

> State and society do not acknowledge and has not allowed the same sex relationship of women. Through the same sex relationship, we are fighting for social and legal recognition for to enjoy the marital life and established the family.

So, various factors play important role to push an individual to live in live-in relationship. These factors include rising literacy, information and fictitious thought and search of romantic love relationship, not clear for lifelong commitment but searching a sex partner, urbanization which provide the sense of privacy, freedom and hidden space for relationship, education system which always teach the sense of freedom and sometimes separate from the traditional family setting, mass migration and high division of labour isolate the individual, limitation of legal provision; on a same sex relationship, double partnership, early age marriage. Some of these causes are interconnected to each other. We are unable to declare which factors are prominent and which factors are less important without conducting detail research.

CONCLUSION

Marriage, a pivotal social institution, has evolved from a normative union between a man and a woman for procreation and life-sharing to a more complex concept influenced by socio-cultural rights, responsibilities and philosophical ideologies. Traditionally, marriage was seen as a permanent, monogamous bond, often criticized from Marxist and feminist perspectives as oppressive, particularly towards women. Restrictions on sexual relationships outside of marriage, especially for women, were symbolized by practices like the Sati system and the wearing of white in Christian weddings, reflecting societal notions of purity.

The rise of science and technology, alongside the capitalist mode of production, has led to a re-evaluation of these norms, with increasing acceptance of living together, same-sex relationships, single parenthood, divorce, and remarriage. This shift reflects a broader societal transformation from well-known communal living to a more individualistic existence.

Sociological theories offer diverse lenses to analyse marriage. Marxism views it as an oppressive institution that should be abolished; feminism aligns with this view, highlighting the patriarchal control over women; structural functionalism emphasizes marriage's role in social cohesion and order; and modernism focuses on rationality and the evolution of societal functions.

Marx and Engels, in their Communist Manifesto, argued that the bourgeois family structure, based on capital and private gain, would disappear with capitalism. Later developments in Europe, particularly after the fall of communist governments, saw a decline in marriage rates and a rise in cohabitation and births outside of marriage, suggesting that communism did not mandate the abolition of marriage.

Modernism posits that the weakening of religious control over individuals, particularly regarding sexuality, has led to a more liberal approach to relationships. Pope Francis's recognition of cohabiting couples and the liberal political thought advocating for personal relationships beyond traditional marriage further illustrate this trend.

In summary, marriage as an institution is undergoing significant changes, reflecting the dynamic interplay between socio-cultural norms, legal frameworks, and philosophical thought. This article aims to provide a theoretical understanding of marriage and analyse the global and situation in Nepal, considering various sociological theories and critiques.

NOTES

1. Sati is a wife burning system after the death of her husband. In 1977 government of Nepal officially banned this system.
2. In Hindu religious society, widow women are not allowed to make makeup, use bangle, wear read coloured cloth and vermilion in forehead. Widowed women also do not have the right to remarry, if she does remarry, she and her children are deducted from the caste status.
3. And also Christianity not allowed the sexual desire of women Clare Chambers write on her article 'The Marriage Free State' (2013) that 'The white wedding is replete with sexist imagery the father 'giving away' the bride; the white dress symbolizing the bride's virginity and emphasizing the importance of her appearance; the vows to obey the husband; the minister telling the husband 'you may now kiss the bride' (rather than the bride herself giving permission, on indeed initiating or at least equally participating in the act of kissing); the reception at which, traditionally, all the speeches are given by men; 'the wife surrendering her own name and taking her husband's'.
4. Now citizenship right became a constitutional right but in a practice the registration of child was unable to register without the marriage certificate of their parents. Various parents now get married to registered their children's birth certificate at Government record.
5. In European and American context live-in relationship is known as Cohabitation and often it came as synonym in cited literature. I want to declare it that the term 'cohabitation' and the living together is a same in this thesis. like, 'cohabitation', 'living apart relationship', 'live-in relationship', 'civil union', 'civil partnership', 'intimate care giving union' (ICGU)'.
6. This feature news was published at one of few authentic online portals called *Setopati* in 27 August 2023 based on the case studies and the Key Informant Interview provided by Women Commission of Nepal. In Women Commission, women came to register the case of domestic or sexual violence. In the process of discussion to register the file, they share their relationship as living together which are not legally recognized. https://www.setopati.com/social/310290
7. The death story of Safina Miya, who was in a live-in relationship but after some misunderstanding she was killed. https://www.onlinekhabar.com/2024/01/1422817?utm_source=Facebook& utm_medium= FBpage1 &fbclid=IwAR13JiNx13yCHvb6QhzVfVnDV3W80ln-rfqVf9WwRGWaYOeol73q3ckrqB0

8. The killing of RojinaTamanghttps://ekantipur.com/national/2023/06/07/1684825224994939996.html
9. Story of death of Unisha Rai and Anish Jimi https://ekantipur.com/national/2022/01/07/164155822169968243.html
10. Case of X (who live with her boyfriend), was suffered from domestic violence by her boyfriend. She tried to file the case against her boyfried in police office, Nepal Police denied to file the case and she publicly post her statement at face book. It's highly debatable in social media.
11. Case story 'Y' who are actor suicide and there is news he was living together with her girlfriend and they are acting in same film.
12. Case 'Z', Famous singer was in the live-in relationship. After the birth of child, he started to ignore his partner and child at the time of early motherhood, he used to beat her and his partner file the case and got marital status.
13. Senior Lawyer Shashi Adhikari answer on her interview on TV show that when to people are in live-in relationship they hide their relationship, when they suffered or feel threat from relationship, they bring the relation on public sphere either with police case or asking support from NGOs or direct case file in court. https://www.youtube.com/watch?v=bkk_p-ulDBk
14. On 14 March 2024 Advocate Annu Bhattarai file the petition at Supreme Court demanding the legal status for live-in relationship. In this petition she claims that if the government formulate a legal foundation to living together divorce rate will be reducing with the reduction of physical, mental violence and destruction of social structure. https://newsgriha.com/detail/18442

REFERENCES

Achhami, Sarisha (2023). *Women File the Case that 'He Didn't Marry Me After Live-in Relationship': Do Not Have Evidence, Do Not Have Law. Setopati,* 27 August 2023. https://www.setopati.com/social/310290

Beauvoir, Simon De (1953). *Second Sex.* London: Vintage.

Bumpass, Larry L, James A. Sweet and Andrew Charlin, (1991). The Role of Cohabitation in Declining Rate of Marriage. *Journal of Marriage and Family.* November 1991, vol. 53, no. 4.

Chambers, Clare (2013). 'The Marriage Free State'. *Proceedings of the Aristotelian Society*: Oxford: Oxford University Press.

Dahal, Bishnu Prasad (2020). Living Together Relationship: Towards A New Pattern of Adult Life in Kathmandu. *International Journal of Social Science and Human Research*, vol. 3, pp. 191-201.

Engels, Frederick (translator: Alec West) 1993 (1972). *The Origin of the Family, Private Property and the State*. New York: International Publishers.

Formation, Lenka and Alena Krizkova (2015). Love Will Keep Us Apart? Understanding Living Apart Together Partnerships in the Post state-socialist Czech Republic. *Czech Sociological Review*, vol. 51, no. 6, Special Issue: Gender Aspects of the Life Course.

Friedan, Betty (1963). *The Feminine Mystique*. New York: Penguin.

Ghimire J. Dirgha et al. (2006). Social Change, Premarital Nonfamily Experience, and Spouse Choice in an Arranged Marriage Society, *AJS Volume* 111 number 4. Chicago: The University of Chicago.

Kenney, Catherine T. and Sara S. Mclanahan (2006). Why are Cohabiting Relationships More Violent than Marriage. *Demography*, February 2006, vol. 43, no. 1.

Mainali, Sujit (2021). *Sati*. Kathmandu: Kitab.

Marx, Karl and Frederick Engels (1848, 1872, 2021). *The Communist Manifesto*. Kathmandu: Educational Book House.

Nguyen Trung, Kien (2018). From Sociology of the Family to Sociology of Personal Life: A Review of the Literature. *Sociology*, vol. 6, no. 2, Institute of Sociology, Hanoi: Vietnam.

Thami, Tekraj (2024). Crime Produce by Extramarital Affair: Living Together in Trust, Killing in Debate. *Nayapatrika*, 22 January 2024. https://www.nayapatrikadaily.com/news-details/133011/2024-01-22

Thornton, Arland (2009). Sweeping Changes in Marriage, Cohabitation, and Childbearing in Central and Eastern Europe: New Insights from the Developmental Idealism Framework, *European J. Popul.* 2009; 25(2).

Tönnies, Ferdinand (1957). *Community and Society (Gemeinschaft und Gesellschaft)*. East Lansing: The Michigan State University Press.

Waal, Anastasia de (2008). Cohabitation. *An Irish Quarterly Review*. Spring 2008, vol. 97, no. 385.

CHAPTER 6

Security Insights from the Buddhist Principles in the 1910 BS (1854 AD) *Muluki Ain**

SHIVA PRASAD PAUDEL

HINDU SCRIPTURES WERE THE FUNDAMENTAL SOURCE OF STATE LAW

In ancient Nepal, when it was ruled by *Kirats*, the *Mundhum*, a religious text of *Kiratis*, was believed to have ruled the country. (Wasti(1) 5). However, there was not adequate evidence of whether *Mundhum* was a normative standard or in practice. Some historians argue that *Mundhum* was the basis of day to day ruling of the society. *Mundhum* has a chapter of *Kharom Thim*, which deals with the system of justice (Wasti(1) 20).

In the time of *Lichhavis*, there was no reference to one law or code. The existing historical evidence are inscriptions alone. Most of them underline the establishment of *Guthi* (endowments of land) for the operation of *Vihars* and the performance of religious rites. These *Guthis* were kept for conducting pujas of Hindu and Buddhist Temples and for maintenance and operation of Hindu and Buddhist Temples and Buddhist *Sangha* and *Vihars* (monasteries).[1]

* This paper was presented at a seminar of academics and students at Lumbini Buddhist University on 10-11 March 2024 at Lumbini, Nepal.

In medieval Nepal, *Jayasthiti Malla* enacted a code, called *Manav Nyayashastra*. This *Nayashastra* is based on the Hindu belief system. (Wasti 21). It has referred to Hindu rituals, such as *yagya* (fire rituals), *dana* (donation) and the Hindu *Varna* system. It has quoted *Narad Rishi* and claimed that the code consists of dharmas propounded by *Dharmadev*. (*Manav Nyayashastra*, Wasti(2) 270). However, the account of the transaction, etc. also reflects that some of its provisions on property management and marriage were the insertion of the local customs and practices rather than the direct instructions of Hindu scriptures (*dharmasastras*). Balaram Kayastha has noted that Jayasthiti Malla cannot be entirely accused of destroying *Buddhism* in the valley. He was a devout Hindu practitioner but respectful of other religions. The restoration of *Swyambhunath Chaitya* after the attack of *Shamsuddin* was carried out in his time (Kayastha 141).

The rulers of Gorkha were also Hindus and they also adhere to the *Varna* system. The *Thitis* (a kind of royal decree) issued by Ram Shah mentions the enforcement of the *Varna* system (*Muluki Ain* 1910 BS: Annex 1). The appointment of *Brahmins* as *Rajgurus*, provision of *danas* (gifts) to *Brahmins*; and prohibition of capital punishment to *Brahmins* were specifically reflected in his *Thitis*. Prithvi Narayan Shah spent most of his life conquering other kingdoms, his ideas and values are reflected in his divine advice (*Divya Upadesha*). His *Divya Upadesha* reflects that he was an ardent Hindu devotee and he also instructed to keep a pundit/priest in every court to dispense justice as per the *Nyayashastra*/scripture). His advice clearly instructs the rulers and citizens to follow the traditions and religion (*Kula Dharma*) of their forefathers (*Divya Upadesha*, Wasti1 76, 81).

Rana Bahadur Shah's *sawal* of 1863 BS reinforces the caste system, forbids the killing of cows (except *Chauri*, i.e. *mount Ain cow/ Yak/Nak*) and marriage against the established social practice (*nachalyakorit*). The *sawal* (a royal decree) of 1863 prohibited to destruction of the rest house of travellers (*pati-pauwa*), the religious site (*dewal*) and the footbridge (*sanghu*) (*Rana Bahadur Shah ko Bandobasta*, Wasti1 76). Another piece of legislation before the *Ain* of 1910 BS was the Bandej (a typical form of administrative law) of Ujir Singh Thapa (Governor of Palpa Gauda/area), dated 1879 BS. In this *Bandej*, he had specifically mentioned that if someone unintentionally does an unlawful sexual act, which takes away his or her caste, s/he should be pardoned as per the scriptures (*dharmashastra*). (Fourth Bandej, nos. 17 and 20, Wasti(1) 105). This means that he is referring to the Hindu *dharmashastra* which provisions for the *Varna* system. However, his *bandej* also clearly mentions that adhering to the customs is not punishable, such as a marriage between cousins through maternal uncle and paternal aunt.[2] (Fourth Bandej no. 19, Wasti(1)).

It is clear from the royal decree issued by *Ram Shah*, a royal order of *Prithvi Narayan Shah* and the administrative order issued by Ujir Singh Thapa that customary law was made part of the Nepalese legal order. However, a detailed study is yet to be carried out to what extent the provisions of Hindu scriptures were modified and customary laws got a greater space into the Nepalese legal system. Making an exception of killing *cauri* (Yak) from the offense of killing cows is a good example of such modification.

THE (*MULUKI*) *AIN* OF 1910 BS: THE FIRST COMPREHENSIVE CODE BASED ON HINDU SCRIPTURES AND CUSTOMARY PRACTICES

The (*Muluki*) *Ain* or the National Code, 1854,[3] (hereinafter the *Ain*) ruled the country until it was replaced by the new *Muluki Ain* of 2020 BS (1963 AD).[4] The Prime Minister Jung Bahadur Kunwar Rana was the main initiator behind this codification (Wasti 25) (Khatiwoda 3). Wasti has named *Lokpati Jha* and *Leshpati Jha* as drafters of the Ain (Wasti 25). The *Ain* was discussed in the council of 219 office-bearers and was issued with their names printed in the preamble. The e-copy published by the Nepal Law Commission has included three royal orders issued by Shree Panch Prithvi Bir Bikram Shah Dev. The second royal order of 1943 BS records a major revision of the Ain in the same year. This rewriting was not only made to remove the repetitions but also to include well-established practices and customs into law.[5] This order also allows the prime minister and the council to make changes in the law as per the customs and practices. Earlier to this date, two royal orders of 1910 BS and 1942 BS did not have any content to allow the prime minister and the council to accommodate the customs and practice into the law.

The *Ain* had regulated civil matters such as property, cash transactions, wages, adoption and marriage; criminal matters- such as gambling, witchcraft, rape, sexual intercourse, incest, murder and maintenance of caste-based-order; and *Dharmadhikar*, court procedure and evidential matters.

The preamble emphasizes the equal application of the law among people of the same caste, while formally accepting different treatment of individuals belonging to different castes as a legal principle. Thus, the Nepalese polity until 1963 was accused of ruling based on the Hindu belief system,[6] which reinforces caste-based social order, non-killing of *Brahmins*, cows and women, etc. Despite the claim, the *Ain* fails to prescribe the comprehensive list of four *Varna*s and the six castes and their subgroups. Khatiwoda et al. have counted that the *Ain* has referred to sixty-three castes besides the castes within the Newar community (around twenty-six castes within Newar alone) and approximately seven ascetic groups (Khatiwoda 29). There could be two reasons for this anomaly. The first one is that the *Varna* system was developed in the southern plains long ago and they were ignorant of the diversity between people that existed in the northern Himalayan range and other far-off places. The second reason could be that over time practices of drinking alcohol and eating meat developed even within some communities, including *Khasa*, which traditionally fall either in *Brahmin* or Chhetri communities (Khatiwoda 30).

Interestingly, the four classifications of people among Hindu Scriptures—*Brahmin*, *Kshetriya* or *Chhetris*, *Vaishya* and *Sudra*, are not found in the Ain. The primary classification made by the *Ain* is—*tagadhari* (sacred thread-wearers), *matawali* (alcohol-drinkers but touchable and perhaps water-acceptable), and (fully) untouchable caste. Muslims and Christians were put under touchable but not water-acceptable castes. The *Ain* has used the term 'European' at a place and '*mleccha*' at a couple of other places, which seems to mean Christians only.[7] Except for one provision, which shall be discussed in another section, other provisions where Muslims, Christians and Europeans are mentioned for offenses, such as illicit sexual intercourse; protection from violence such as beating, being sold by the husband and goods that can be touched by Muslims and Christians.

The *Ain* is not entirely the reinforcement of Hindu practices. It has also given some space, though it looks contradictory to the modern belief system and customary practices. For example, the *Ain* has given the freedom to people to choose their livelihood as a cobbler, tailors and other forms of labour work.[8] From Hindu *Dharmashastra's* point of view, such acts should be prohibited for upper castes such as *Brahmin*s and *Chhetris.*

SPECIFIC PROVISIONS ON THE DHARMIC PRACTICES OF NON-HINDU TRADITIONS AND ASCETICS WITHIN HINDU TRADITION

The *Ain* has a few provisions that can be interpreted to allow the customary practices of non-Hindu religions. However, the *Ain* are careful in preventing Hindu ascetics or non-householders from expanding their constituency.

In the chapter of *Dharmadhikar*, it is very affirmatively stated that all four castes including Muslims and Europeans can 'perform any act that is in accordance with their family traditions and beliefs and leads to Dharma' except slaughtering the cow.[9] The *Ain* criminalizes an act of disturbance on the performance of such a dharmic act. This provision is very broad to provide everyone including Christians and Muslims to carry out tasks according to their family tradition.

There is only one direct Buddhist reference in the *Ain*, which does not read encouraging. Section 35 of the chapter on *Dharmadhikar* reads as follows:

> When hearing the mantra (i.e., during the initiation), the members of Sacred Thread-wearing castes, including *Brahmin*s and those belonging to Alcohol-drinking castes for whom it is customary to receive the initiation,

shall hear and recite the mantra given by their guru according to their own tradition as followed by their fathers and forefathers (purkha). If they do not recite the mantra according to their own tradition as followed by their fathers and forefathers and follow the Buddhist path or any [other] atheistic *jhanna-panna* doctrine 411, a fine of 50 rupees shall be imposed on them. If they have themselves consumed cooked rice from a follower of the *jhanna-panna* doctrine and if they have also contaminated others [by feeding them cooked rice], their share of property shall, in accordance with the Ain, be confiscated. Their sacred thread shall be removed and they shall be degraded from their caste status.[10]

The above section can be divided into three parts. The first part promotes the continuation of the practice of receiving initiation and hearing and reciting *mantras*, which was carried out by their fathers and forefathers as a tradition. The emphasis was on the continuation of the same tradition without any alteration. Hence, the importance is given to the exact *mantras* given by the guru or the master. This practice is not only limited to the sacred thread-wearer but also to all the members where such tradition existed. The second part is applicable in a condition where a Hindu refuses to recite the *mantra* and converts to Buddhism or any other atheistic religion. In such case, one shall be imposed a fine. In the third part, one must lose property and caste, if one becomes a follower of the *jhanna-panna* doctrine together with eating the rice cooked by other followers and feeding the same to others.

Another provision of the *Ain* also prohibits a sacred-thread-wearer householder from hearing *mantras*[11] primarily from the non-householder person or *Fakir*, which includes *Sannyasi*, *Vairagi*, *Nanaka*, *Kanaphatta*, *Jogi*, *Jangam* or *Sebada*. If a householder hears the *mantra* from these *Fakirs* or accepts them as their *guru*, he shall be fined (The chapter on *Dharmadhikar*, section 36). Likewise, these eight and other robe-wearers are prohibited to convert anyone with force or lure. Only persons above sixteen (including widows) were allowed to be converted into these practices if they wished. [The chapter on conversion to ascetics (*Fakirsita Mudinya*)]. The *Ain* notes that there were three kinds of *Fakirs*—one is the wanderer without anything, the second has the religious institution and the third one has the house and property. The *Ain* has prescribed separate punishment for these three types of *Fakir*s for making conversion [The chapter on conversion to ascetics (*Fakirsita Mudinya*), section 1]. In the context of death-related purification (*Aasouch Barne*), the *Ain* accepts the presence of *Brahmacarin* (celibate) in the then society but does not deal with it any further.

There are several references to above mentioned eight groups of *Sannyasi*, etc. and many other robe-wearers in the *Ain* but none of these provisions indicate that these renouncers were from the Buddhist faith. Such unclear provisions can be interpreted both in favour or against the Buddhist practitioner.

In the wake of having no provision in the *Ain* prohibiting customary religious practice, it can be stated that the Buddhist population or any other population can continue with their customary practices. However, if the Buddhist practice requires to carry out conversion of laity or people from other religions to the Buddhist path, this seems to have been prohibited by the *Ain*. The scheme of prohibition to conversion is not only applied to Buddhists but also to the other ascetic paths that traditionally fall under Hindus as well.

However, it is reasonable to accept that the *Ain* does not deal with the Buddhist *Bajracaryas* and the rest of the Buddhist *Newars* (Khatiwada, 33). It is also reasonable to state that the *Ain* neither wished to highlight the Buddhist practices of Kathmandu valley and elsewhere by putting a separate chapter nor risked forbidding these century-long practices.

The administrative power of the Buddhist *Sangha* has not been recognized by the State since the time of *Manav Nyayashastra*. It cannot be said that the administrative power of *Sangha* mentioned in the inscription of *Pashupatinath-Vajraghar* was an exception or a mainstream practice.

ESTABLISHMENT OF GUTHI AND CHARITABLE ENDOWMENTS: A UNIQUE AND ESSENTIAL FEATURE OF NEPALESE RELIGIOUS PRACTICE

The establishment and maintenance of *Guthi* have been an important feature of the promotion of religious and cultural practices in

Nepal. It is well known that the *Lichhavis* had kept several *Guthis* for the pujas of temples and maintenance of *Sangha* and *Vihars.*[12] Mostly in the times of Mallas, the inscription suggests the maintenance and restoration of the Buddhist and Hindu Temples and donation to public works, such as making wells and rest-house for travellers (*pati-pauwas*).[13]

The *Ain* has promoted the establishment of *Guthi* on Nepali soil and forbids establishment of *Guthi* in Indian religious places, namely, Kashi and Kedar. It provides two factual accounts of the confiscation of a Royal *Guthi* established by Rana Bahadur Shah and the denial of protection of the right to land and *Shivalaya* and a *Dharmashala* built in it by a former prime minister by the British India Government (The chapter on *Datta Guthi*, section 1). The *Ain* presents that Nepal has significant religious sites compared to India. It acclaims the high religious purity of Nepal by describing it as the only Hindu Kingdom in the *Kali* era. It praises the piousness of the country having *Jyotirmaya Shree Pashupatinath* and *Shree Guheshwori* and proclaims Nepal as a sacred place (*punya bhumi*). It clearly states the protection of Royal *Guthi* established from the time of Dravya Shah but does not refer to the protection of *Guthi* established before the Shah period. (The chapter on *Datta Guthi*, section 5). The *Ain* fails to recognize the historic contribution made by the Kings of Kathmandu Valley and other parts of Nepal in ancient and medieval times. Likewise, the *Ain* also does not admire the religious sanctity of Buddhist chaityas or shrines. Khatiwoda et al. have argued that '*(t)*he legal recognition of *Guthi* land can even be read as the integration of different (divine) forms of spatiality embedded in the state space' (Khatiwoda 27), however, there is no specific reference to Buddhist stupas, chaityas that existed in the Himalayan, Hill and Terai region. Even if you believe that the rulers had a deep respect for Buddhist deities, that is not reflected in the black letter of the *Ain.*

Nonetheless, several provisions in the *Ain* protect the *Guthi* that were established from the time of fathers, forefathers and ancestors (The chapter on *Datta Guthi*, sections. 6-27).

The *Ain* promotes *Guthi* both for temples and other public works, etc., and charitable endowment (*sadabarta*) for *paupers* and

Fakirs, etc. (the chapter on *Datta Guthi*, section 2). Khatiwoda et al. summarize the provisions in the *Ain* that highlight mainly three primary purposes for establishing *Guthi* and charitable endowment: religious and ritual purposes, such as the maintenance of Shiva temples, pilgrim's refuges (*Dharamsala*) and the performance of compulsory, occasional or annul worship of deities (*nitya-* and *naimittika-puja*) (the chapter on *Datta Guthi*, section 1); welfare purposes, such as the daily distribution of meals to orphans, elderly people without family or disabled persons [the chapter on Poor (pauper), section 6] or the arrangement of funeral ceremonies (the chapter on Funerals, section 5); and, finally, the maintenance of public facilities, such as wayside shelters, fountains, bridges, ghatas, wells, ponds, paths, resting places or gardens (the chapter on Making Houses, section 9) (Khatiwoda 51).

The *Ain* documents the Nepalese tradition of establishing *Guthi* being carried out by Kings and Citizens from ancient times. However, there seems to be a difference in the trend. In the time of *Lichhavis* and Mallas, the *Guthis* were established for the performance of puja, maintenance of the temple and Buddhist Sangha. However, the *Ain* promotes charitable endowments for paupers and mendicants.

The Act has not failed to prescribe the protective measures to upkeep the *Guthi* as well as the punishment for harming *Guthi*. It prescribes that if kings and ministers confiscate *Guthi* or don't give a replacement of *Guthi* land when confiscated, they will accumulate demerits (*paap*) and open the door to hell (The chapter on *Datta Guthi*, sections 1 and 25). The *Ain* established a separate administrative body (the *Guthi* Janch Adda) and a special court (the *Guthi* Kancahari) for the upkeeping of endowments (The chapter on Poor, section 6). Such offices were not known to have been established in the ancient or medieval period.

SOME OTHER CONSIDERATIONS TO INTERPRET THE *MULUKI AIN* OF 1910 BS

The following two considerations are important to get a balanced picture of the reality before and during the time of *Ain*.

The Contribution of Shah Kings to the Preservation of Buddhist Practices

There can be no doubt that the Shah Kings were Hindus. However, the words of Prithvi Narayan Shah, who is the founder of modern Nepal, did not have a policy of suppressing the customs and practices that were in operation from the time of their fathers and forefathers. It is said that he ordered the continuation of the *Samyak Mahadan*, which was discontinued after his victory over Kathmandu Valley and imposed a fine on those who refused to participate. He also did not stop any Buddhist religious festivals in Kathmandu Valley. Rana Bahadur Shah was known to have performed the puja of *Mahamaya Bhairavi* in accordance with a Boudha tantra. He also donated land to a Tibbetan Lama to establish a *Guthi* in 1786 AD. He also permitted the Tibetan Lama to establish the Dev Dharma Monastery and a temple of Mother Harati (Ghimire 144).

Surendra Bikram Shah is also known to have constructed a chaitya and put idols of *Vajrapani* and *Dipankar* in the *Chaitya* in *Yatkha Bahal*, Kathmandu. After the establishment of democracy in 2007 BS, King Tribhuvan visited *Anandakuti Vihar* on Buddha *Jayanti*. He was the kind who declared a national holiday on the day of Buddha *Purnima*.

Swaym bhunath Mahachaitya went under several renovations over a couple of centuries. For sure, a couple went under the Rana rule. Ranas did not oppose a major renovation which took place in the time of Rajendra Bir Bikram Shah (Shakya 2004).

Rana Regime's Prosecution of Theravada Monks

Xuanzang or Hiuen Tsang, in his travel account of the second half of the seventh century, also mentions his visit to two places in the present Nepal the country of Kapilvastu and the country of Nepal.[14] (Li Rongxi 145, 171). Visiting Kapilvastu he mentions the condition of two palace cities which were completely deserted. In relation to the Buddhist practice, he writes '(t)here are more than one thousand ruined foundations of old monasteries and beside the palace city is a monastery inhabited by over three thousand monks, who study the Hinayana teachings of the *Sammitiya* school.

There are two deva temples, with heretics (Hindu) living together' (Li Rongxi 152). Regarding his impression of Kathmandu valley, he mentions '(*t*)he monasteries and deva temples are so close together that they touch each other and there are more than two thousand monks, who study both Mahayana and Hinayana teachings' (Li Rongxi 192). It is also believed that out of nine missionary groups commissioned by King Asoka to propagate Buddhism in different places, one group of four monks led by Ven. Majjima came to Nepal and succeeded in propagating Buddhism in Nepal. It is popularly believed that Theravada Buddhism in practiced during Asoka's time, which was also spread to Nepal. Unfortunately, for some unknown reason, the popularity of Buddhism declined and Vajrayana became the main Buddhist practice in Kathmandu Valley.[15]

An attempt at its resurgence took place in the early twentieth century but without success. In 1924 CE (1990 BS), Nanikaji Shrestha (known as Mahapragya), with other four monks—*Mahachandra*, *Mahagyan*, *Mahavriya* and *Mahaksanti*, wearing Buddhist robes, went on to the street of Kathmandu for alm collection. It was an unusual scene in the Kathmandu Valley. Prime Minister Chandrashamser exiled these five Buddhists for the crime of converting themselves to Buddhism (Ghimire 139). Mahapragya Nanikaji Shrestha together with another Bhikshu Amritananda (Lalkaji Shakya) came to *Bhojpur* from the Indian side to preach Buddhism in 1927 CE. The chief administrator (*Badahakim*) of the region arrested Mahapragya after learning that he was formally exiled by the government. They were exiled again to India upon receiving the order of Prime Minister Juddha Shamser (Ghimire 140).

However, these exiled Bhikshus did not give up. They organized themselves under the leadership of Bhikshu Amritananda. They mobilized international Buddhist communities to persuade the Nepalese government for allowing Buddhist practices. Bhikshu Amritananda was finally successful in establishing the first Theravada Bouddha Vihar in *Swyambhunath* in 1948 CE with the permission of the time of Prime Minister Mohan Shamser. Prime Minister Mohan Shamsher also permitted to give an official holiday to Buddhist followers on the day of Buddha *Purnima* (Ghimire 142).

CONCLUSION

The *Ain* uses the term 'Buddhist' only in one place. The use of the term also does not favour the promotion of Buddhist faith. However, it would be unsuitable to conclude that Buddhist practices were forbidden by the State. The account of *Hiuen Tsang* records the decline of Buddhism in the *Kapilvastu* area. Balaram Kayastha has also noted that *Jayasthiti Malla* cannot be entirely accused of destroying *Buddhism* in the valley.

It is well-established that the Buddhist religious practices started from the *Lichhavi* period. Hence, this was already established as the customary practice before the promulgation of the *Ain*. Hence, most (if not all) of the Buddhist practices should be well-protected under the recognition of customary religious practices under the *Ain*. Buddhist scriptures do not support killing in general and therefore the prohibition of cows cannot be interpreted as an interference with their religious practice. In terms of the public preaching of Buddhism, which has been an established practice since the time of Gautam Buddha seems not to be favoured by the *Ain*. The exile of Theravadin monks by the Rana regime in 1924 and 1927 AD, indicating the ban on Buddhist propagation can be interpreted as the suppression of Buddhist practices. The permission for the establishment of Anandakuti Vihar in 1948 can be taken as the beginning of the Theravadin practice in Nepal. Regarding, Himalayan or Mahayana Buddhism, their practice was not known to be interrupted by the Rana regime. They had legal protection under the rule of customary practice and their activities were also mostly unnoticed by the central administration.

Adopting the policy of promotion of the *Guthi* system by the *Ain* can be interpreted as non-interference to the established religious practice of Buddhism. This benefitted in continuing the practices of Buddhism. The donation or offering, though limited, made by the Kings and Ranas directly for the pujas, maintenance and renovation of Buddhist *Chaityas* and approval of offerings by other donors to maintain and renovate the *Chaityas* during the time of the *Ain*, does underline that the public policy was not against the Buddhist practice.

Though the *Ain* failed to include Nepal's Buddhist glory in its text, neither Ranas nor Shahs were known to have suppressed any customary Buddhist practices. They might have made very little financial contribution but they were known to discourage the contributors as well. Nonetheless, we could sense from the reading of *Muluki Ain* that Buddhist communities must have had a tremendous struggle to avoid the cloud of fear hanging above them.

NOTES

1. *Infra* note 13.
2. This rule has continued to the *Muluki Ain* of 1910 BS (see, the chapter on Marriage, section 18). Likewise, the recognition of customary practices of Killing a wife's adulterer also continued in the Ain of 1910 BS (see, the chapter on Adultery to a Woman from Enslaveable Caste, section 12 and most of the provisions in the chapter on Miscellaneous Regulations Concerning Adultery).
3. The author reviewed the *Muluki Ain*, 1910 BS published by the Nepal Law Commission on its website as of 30 January 2024. This version of the *Muluki Ain* is not the original copy but with several amendments. (Wasti 25). Annex-Chha (7) of the document states that it was issued in the reign of Shree Panch Prithvi Bir Bikram Shah Dev and Prime Minister Shree Teen Chandra Shamser in 1958 BS. The annexes Cha and Chha (6 and 7) state that the first amendment was made in 1943 BS in the reign of Shree Panch Prithvi Bir Bikram Shah Dev and Prime Minister Shree Teen Bir Shamser. However, Wasti has claimed that the *Ain* was amended several times. It is pertinent to mention that when originally enacted, it did not receive the name *Muluki*. The addition of *Muluki* before the word '*Ain*' was the later development (Wasti 25).
4. The preamble of the Ain also mentions the names of three generations of Kings chiefly Shree Panch Rajendra Bir Bikram Shah Dev and Trailokya Bir Bikram Shah Dev. The scheme was to endorse the Ain by the former King and the crown prince (Wasti 25) and (Khatiwoda 3).
5. It is not definite which was the Hindu belief system or which was the actual practice developed in Nepal. However, some authors have argued that the *Muluki Ain* of 1854 codified customary law (Khatiwoda 2). A detailed analysis is yet to happen to what extent the scriptures were applied and to what extent they were modified.

6. A researcher has given a few examples of how the *Manusmrti* made its way to the Ain. (Khatiwoda1 6-18).
7. For the use of the term European, *see* the chapter on *Dharmadhikar*. For the use of the term Christian, see the chapter on Drinking Liquor and Untouchability. For the use of the term *Mleccha*, see the chapter on *Dharmadhikar*, section 38; the chapter on Miscellaneous Regulations Concerning Adultery, section 2; the chapter on Illicit Sexual Intercourse with Water-unacceptable Castes, section 1; and the chapter on Untouchable Class, section 17. For the use of the term Muslims, *see* the chapter on Beating between Father and Son, section 19; the chapter on Selling the Wife, secs. 1 and 2; the chapter on Drinking Liquor and Untouchability, section 2; the chapter on *Dharmadhikar*, section 38; the chapter on Miscellaneous Regulations Concerning Adultery, section 2; the chapter on Illicit Sexual Intercourse with Water-unacceptable Castes, sections 1 and 6; the chapter on Miscellaneous Regulations Concerning Adultery, sec. 2; the chapter on Illicit Sexual Intercourse with Water-unacceptable Castes, sections 1, 4, 5, 6 and the bottom table of the chapter on Untouchable Castes. Muslims and Christians have been designated as water-unacceptable but touchable castes. (Khatiwoda 32).
8. The chapter on Choosing a Profession, section 7.
9. The translation was by Khatiwoda et al. (Khatiwoda 490). *See* the chapter of *Dharmadhikar*, section 1.
10. Ibid., 502.
11. Khatiwoda et al. have stated that this provision applies while hearing the *mantra* during initiation. However, the plain text of the *Ain* does not indicate so. The *mantra* reciting practices are the established practice in Hinduism and can take place on other occasions as well.
12. Inscription in *Lichhavi* period compiled by (Bajracharya1): Guthi(s) in *Swyambhu* (pp. 384-5), *Dhokatol* (p. 386), Lalitpur-Chapa Tole and Kantipur-*Musumbahal* (p. 507), *Sankhu* (508), Patan-Mangalbazar-Bhimsen Mandir (p. 454), Pashupati-*Vajraghar* (pp. 499-506), Handigaun (p. 320).
13. Pre-medieval or later *Lichhavi* period inscription by (Bajracharya 2): *Sankhu Vajrayogini* (p. 37), Lalitpur-*Kumbheswor* (p. 229), Lalitpur *Pimbahal* (pp. 150-1), *Swyambhu* (p. 157), etc.
14. (Li Rongxi 145, 171). The Great Tang Dynasty Record of the Western Regions, Bukkyo Dendo Kyokai and Numata Center for Buddhist Translation and Research, Berkeley.
15. https://web.archive.org/web/20140804160554/http://www.lumbini.org.uk/bd_n_thera_t.html.

REFERENCES

Bajracharya, Dhanavajra (1), *Licchavikalin* Abhilekh (Inscription from the *Lichhavi* Period), Center for Nepal and Asian Studies, TU (2053 BS).

Bajracharya, Dhanavajra (2), Madhyakalin *Licchavi* Abhilekh (Inscription from the Medieval *Lichhavi* Period), Center for Nepal and Asian Studies, TU (2068 BS).

Ghimire, Chandrakala, *Nepalma Buddha Dharmako Itihas* (History of Buddhism in Nepal), Bhunipuran Prakashan (2079 BS).

Kayastha, Balaram, *Prachin the Madhyakalin Nepalko Itihas* (the Ancient and Medieval History of Nepal), Pallav Publication, Nepal (2077 BS).

Khatiwoda, Rajan, Cubelic, Simon, and Michael Axel, The *Muluki Ain* of 1854 (English Translation), Heidelberg University Publishing, (2023 CE).

Li Rongxi, The Great Tang Dynasty Record of the Western Regions, Bukkyo Dendo Kyokai and Numata Center for Buddhist Translation and Research, Berkeley (1996 AD).

Muluki Ain, 1910 BS (Nepali Copy), Nepal Law Commission.

Shakya, Min Bahadur, *Sri Swayambhu Mahachaitya*, Swayambhu Vikash Mandal, Swayambhu, Kathmandu (2004 AD).

Wasti, Prakash (1), *Kanoon Sambandhi Kehi Aitihasik Abhilekhharu* (Some Historical Documents Related to Law), Kanoon Sahaprakashan (2063 BS).

Wasti, Prakash (2), *Hamro Kanooni Itihaskakehi-Jhankiharu* (Some Pictures of our Legal History), Pairavi Book House (2063 BS).

CHAPTER 7

Third Country Resettlement a 'Tryst with Destiny' of Bhutanese Asylum Seekers in Nepal

SARITA NANDMEHAR

INTRODUCTION

With a population of 8,21,329 (Bhutan Population, 2018), Bhutan has predominantly been a multi-ethnic society. Rich in natural resources including water, Bhutan is one of the countries where the parameter to index the country's growth stands as Gross National Happiness (GNH) unlike Gross Domestic Product (GDP) followed around the world. Considered as one of the happiest and most peaceful places in the world, its past has a different narration of history. Major being the expulsion of the Lohtshampas in the 1990s. While the royal state machinery worked round the clock to ensure their expulsion, it became one of the biggest humanitarian tragedies of the time. Further, it took the shape of a serious ethnic conflict which was rooted in the majority that the Drukpa community's fear had about the domination by the migrant Nepalese Lohtshampas whose population increased phenomenally over the years. To counter this demographic challenge, Drukpa restricted them to the disease-prone southern Bhutan, their movement inside Bhutan and they were not allowed to purchase land and property in other parts of Bhutan (Rose, 1977). As a result, Lohtshampas were isolated socially, culturally and economically isolated.

Bhutan's Lohtshampas are the descendants of peasant farmers from Nepal who began to migrate to southern Bhutan after the

Anglo-Bhutanese war of 1865. Successive generations cleared the forests and formed agrarian communities that quickly became Bhutan's main producers of food. Their numbers were augmented by later migrants, who continued to be brought in by licensed contractors until about 1930. The Nepali settlers became the kingdom's main source of cash income: unlike the Drukpas of the north, who paid their taxes in kind right up until the late 1950s, British colonial records show that Nepali settlers in southwest Bhutan were paying taxes in cash even before the Bhutanese monarchy was established in 1907. Until the 1950s, Bhutan was not a unified polity; different systems of administration were maintained in different parts of the country. In the south, the local contractors and their descendants remained powerful. The revenue raised in certain southern districts was submitted not to the central government but to a local governor based across the Indian border in Kalimpong (Hutt M., 2003, 2005).

In the 1950s, major administrative shuffling took place under the leadership of King Jigme Dorji Wangchuk and Prime Minister Jigme Palden Dorji. Several programmes concerning the development of the country and after due process, these programmes were institutionalized. As a result, a National Assembly was elected under the royal rule and the enforcement of Bhutan's Nationality Law. While the state machinery was institutionalized and their functionaries were clearly defined to protect the ethnic diversity in the country, protecting the rights of minorities was emphasized upon. Also, it was under the 1958 Nationality Law that granted Lohtshampas full citizenship. Meanwhile, to understand the issue of the Lohtshampas, it is relevant to mention the Nationality Law.

The Nationality Law of Bhutan, published in 1958, was reiterated by the Bhutanese government after the 1990s (Hutt M., 2003). In 1958, during the 11th session, the National Assembly of Bhutan enacted the Nationality Act of Bhutan, 1958. It granted the Bhutanese nationality for the first time to all Nepalese who had settled in the Bhutanese Kingdom before 31 December 1958 and applied under naturalization (Hutt M., 2003). Under the following provisions:

1. A person would be considered a Bhutanese national by birth if his/her father was a Bhutanese national, regardless of the person's birth.
2. A foreigner could become a Bhutanese citizen by presenting a petition to an official appointed by His Majesty the Druk Gyalpo and takes an oath of loyalty according to the rules laid down by the official. It again required:
   (a) Resided in Bhutan for more than 10 years, i.e. age of majority.
   (b) Owns agricultural land within the kingdom.
   (c) Has served satisfactorily in government service for at least five years.
3. Foreign wife of a Bhutanese national also required a petition to the king and taking an oath of loyalty.
4. A person could also be deprived of citizenship by becoming citizenship of another country, leaving the country permanently and abandoning the agricultural land (MHA, GoB, 1958).

The government decided to bring the Bhutanese of Nepali origin into the mainstream Drupka culture. The king of Bhutan introduced an ideology of 'One Nation, One People' which led to the imposition of a code of conduct, including Drukpa language, religion and dress for all Bhutanese citizens through a policy of Driglam Namzha (a revival of traditional Bhutanese culture). The primary objective of this policy has been to establish national homogeneity and cohesion among the various linguistic and ethnic groups in the country. In addition to the Driglam Namzha Policy, the government adopted various policies and passed several resolutions in its National Assembly that went against the interest of the Bhutanese of Nepali origin (MHA, GoB, 1958).

In general, the nationality law of 1958 of Bhutan provided three ways to attain citizenship. Firstly, by birth to a father who is a Bhutanese national, secondly, a petition to an official to provide certain conditions of residences and government employment were met and a petition to an official upon marriage to a Bhutanese national. Also, a petition was required on the oath of the loyalty (Hutt M., 2003).

To restrict fresh entries of migrants to Bhutan, the King introduced a new Law in the year 1977. The Citizenship Act of 1985 created more hurdles regarding both the acquisition and termination of citizenship.

THE CENSUS, 1988

The census of 1988 was implemented on the basis of the 1985 citizenship Act. Firstly, the census was conducted by the Bhutanese government only in the five southern districts of Bhutan. Secondly, the authorities excluded ethnic Nepalese from becoming naturalized citizens, as approved for under the 1985 Act.

Instead, the authorities restricted Bhutanese citizenship of ethnic Nepalese who had records, such as tax receipts, to prove residence in Bhutan in 1958, i.e., 30 years before the census. Bhutanese officials refused to accept residency records from the years 1957 and 1959 indicating residency in 1958 to establish citizenship (Human Rights Watch, 2007). They disregarded the citizenship identity cards issued after the previous census: the authorities classified people who could not prove residence in 1958 as non-nationals, 'returned migrants', or other illegal immigrant categories, even if they possessed a citizenship card (Amnesty International, 1994). On the basis of it, people were divided into following categories:

TABLE 7.1: CATEGORY OF MIGRANT

Category	*Type*	*Definition*
F1	Genuine Bhutanese Citizens	–
F2	Returned Migrants	People who left Bhutan and then returned
F3	Drop-out cases	People who were not around at the time of the census
F4	Non-national women married to Bhutanese men and their children	–
F5	Non-national men married to Bhutanese women and their children	–
F6	Adoption cases	Children who are legally adopted and lastly
F7	No nationals	Migrants and illegal settlers

Source: Amnesty International, 1992.

In 1989, the government undertook a survey and realized that the number of Nepali-speaking people was rapidly growing. It led them to adopt a policy called 'Driglam Namzha' or 'One Nation and One People'. Generally, it seems reasonable for a country to adopt such kind of policy but it was not suitable to Bhutan due to the existence of different groups with different cultural practices, religions and languages the government wanted to impose the Nagalong culture, on every citizen.

In 1991, there was a protest against the policy and peaceful demonstration for supporting human rights. But the Voluntary Migration Form were printed in Dzongkha language, which most of the Nepali-speaking people were unable to read. As a result, many who filled it were indirectly giving up their citizenship of Bhutan. This led to the creation of many refugees in Bhutan. Apart from that, the Indian government denied asylum for the Bhutanese refugees and consequently, they had to leave for Nepal and are still remaining in camps since the 1990s.

Though the Royal Government of Bhutan has its own version of the exodus, accounts given by refugees, interviews with refugees' leaders, reports by various human rights organizations and media reports lead us to the conclusion that the exodus of refugees from Bhutan has been broadly in four categories (Kharat, 2007):

- Bhutanese who had been forcefully evicted.
- Bhutanese who had voluntarily emigrated.
- Non-Bhutanese.
- Bhutanese who had committed criminal acts.

Out of these four categories, Thimphu agreed to the return of the people who belonged to the first category, although it felt that most of the refugees in United Nation High Commission for Refugees (UNHCR) camps in eastern Nepal were originally Nepalese and Indian citizens looking for free food and shelter and health care. However, in subsequent bilateral talks, particularly during 1993-6, both Bhutan and Nepal took a more rigid stand regarding the repatriation of Bhutanese refugees (Kharat, 2007).

Till date, in the last 20 years, 15 bilateral talks and many other informal dialogues have taken place. But the government of Bhutan and Nepal could not reach a consensus and conclusion to find a permanent solution. The situation remains unchanged.

The UN convention on Refugees after the cold war in the 1960s and 1980s came into for that reason. However, the repatriation process was adopted in Nepal in 2007. In Article 1 of the statute of UNHCR there are three options for a durable solution:

- Repatriation to the country of origin.
- Rehabilitation in the host country.
- Resettlement in a third country (Refugee Watch Online, 2007).

ROLE OF UNITED NATIONS HIGH COMMISSION FOR REFUGEES

More than 1,30,000 Bhutanese people of Nepali ethnicity have been compelled to live in exile for more than ten years. About 1,00,000 of them live at present in the UNHCR organized refugee camps in Morang and Jhapa districts of eastern Nepal. With the refugee crisis becoming more serious, some of the countries like United States, Canada, Australia, Denmark, Norway, New Zealand and The Netherlands have shown their sympathy and interest in resettling these refugees in their country. In 2006, US Secretary of State Population announced to resettle 60,000 Bhutanese refugees (Human Rights Watch, 2007).

After exhaustive efforts towards repatriation failed, several countries came together, with UNHCR and took initiatives for resettlement of refugees. In November 2007, the government of Nepal publicly accepted and supported for third country resettlement. Thereafter, the Nepal government, UNHCR and the International Organization for Migration and the resettlement countries began resettlement activities. To enjoy the activity and to enjoy the safety of the applicant, prevent threat and violence and anti-resettlement goods, the government established the armed police in the camps by the third country resettlement. UNHCR remains the first way to contact the refugees in order to be eligible for third country resettlement (UNHCR, 2018).

The world food programme works for food, ration and education for the refugees. They undertake the transportation of food in the camps. The Lutheran World Federation distributes the meals to the refugees, every two weeks and the association of medical doctors is responsible for medical services in the camps, CARITAS Australia is responsible for the education of refugee children, Bhutanese refugees serve as team teachers and the curriculum in accordance with the Nepalese public school system and request the livelihood of the repatriation the Bhutanese refugees remaining in Nepal. Although Bhutanese refugees considerably enjoy a bold attitude by the policy of opening camp, technically Bhutanese refugees are not eligible to work, earn property and run a business the situation has remained like this for the past two decades.

At present, many uplifts are found in the refugee camps. The elders and youths wants to return Bhutan to as grounds for hope. They want a quick solution. The elderly have begun to say, 'If our bodies cannot be buried in our motherland, then everything is meaningless.' They are fed up with living for long in troubled camps. They are deprived of citizenship and other political and human rights in Nepal. Moreover, they have bitter experiences and memories of displacement imposed upon them by the autocratic government of Bhutan. Therefore, refugees have a miserable life, are also becoming a real problem for Nepal as their presence in Nepal as a receiving country has led to economic, social, cultural and environmental crisis. The UNHCR and Nepal provided asylum to these refugees on a humanitarian ground.

Resettlement of the Bhutanese refugees in the third country is seen as the only solution, or an option for them as they are fed up with the long run camp lives with deplorable condition. For example, UNHCR staff member Tulsi Limbu was just a child when he saw the refugee arriving in Nepal. He adds:

> I was astonished to see their challenging situation in terms of food and shelter. After spending 20 years in the refugee camps, resettlement is a great option in helping them to start their lives a fresh. I feel very proud that, somewhere, my small efforts were a part of this successful operation (UNHCR, 2013).

On December 1950, the United Nation High Commissioner for Refugees was established by the United Nations General Assembly (UNGA) and it began to officially function on 1 January 1951 with international agencies within the agenda of 'protect and resolve refugee problem' worldwide.

Between the late 1980s and mid-1990s, Bhutan saw the marginalization of its ethnic Nepalese population following protests in the early 1990s. As a result, more than 100,000 ethnic Nepalese fled Bhutan, with the vast majority settling in Nepal. By 1992 the government of Nepal and UNHCR the UN refugee agency had established seven refugee camps in eastern Nepal for the Bhutanese refugees. These camps are among the good refugee's camps in the world, the government of Nepal and UNHCR deserve considerable credit for providing security, shelter, education and health care (UNHCR, 2008).

The Trend Report release, 'UNHCR' shows that at the beginning of 2010 the number of people forcibly displaced worldwide 43.3 million. This is the highest ducat on the mountain. The dramatic thing is not only these numbers are growing but the situation has become more protracted with never-ending conflicts and keeping the people as refugees since the last several decades. The utmost priority to be provided to these people remains shelter. As a brief organization in the field of human displacement UNHCR aims to enter even if these people have lost their home, they haven't lost their future. At the beginning of 2012, more than 26 million people, 10.4 million refugees, 15.6 million IDPs were receiving protection or assistance including shelter from UNHCR.

The Bhutanese refugee's issue being subjected and prioritized as minimal is one of the causes for the long-term non-resolution to the problem which is being done by the Bhutan and Nepal. The news of the 1990 mass demonstration in Bhutan was a surprise to the international community. All of a sudden, the international news media began reporting the physical assault, killings and arbitrary arrest of thousands of people. Henceforth, the Himalayan Kingdom of Bhutan came into focus worldwide.

In the beginning, the international community was not convinced about the true origin of the refugees. Bhutan had stressed that most of those in the camps were either illegal economic immigrants from Bhutan or poor Nepali people gathered from the surrounding areas for assistance by the international relief agencies. It is true in a sense, because one cannot differentiate between the local Nepalese with that of Bhutanese refugees due to similarities in food culture dress language and religion. For the international community, local assimilation would have been the perfect solution. After all, they all are ethnic Nepali people. But, if we see morally, Nepal is unable to afford Bhutanese refugees due to its social and economic problems. Therefore, the durable solution has become widely acceptable to the international community.

UNHCR and other agencies provide a range of services to support refugees in health, education, legal counselling, vocational skills and livelihoods.

Main Objectives

Some 60,000 of Bhutanese refugees in Nepal continuing with the UNHCR, although a number of refugees need protection and assistance. While UNHCR is planning to implement CBDP/TSI (Community Based Development Programme and Transitional Solution Initiatives) with the Government of Nepal and United Nation country team so that it can be implementing for the remaining population of around 34,000 in the host country (UNHCR, 2013).

Favourable Protection Environment

- Access to territory is improved and the risk of refoulement reduced.
- No credible cases of refoulement are reported.

Security from Violence and Exploitation

- The risk of sexual and gender-based violence (SGBV) is reduced and equality of the response to its improved.
- All survivors of SGBV receive support.
- The protection of children is strengthened.

Basic Needs and Essential Services

- The health status of the population is improved.
- All persons of concern have access to primary healthcare.

Durable Solutions

- The potential for resettlement is realized (UNHCR, 2013).

Basic Needs and Assistance

UNHCR is now the world leader in the provision of mass emergency shelter, distribution and delivery. Global coordination on international levels the emergency shelter conduct by UNHCR and IFRC at the country level. UNHCR led the emergency to shelter casting follow conflict, while lifesaving convenient throughout natural disasters.

They are trying to work with International Federation of Red Cross and Red Crescent Societies and other partners as a cluster at the global level. To make sure that the global cluster response is more effective, predictable, and streamlined. In the emergency shelter response, UNHCR main partners are UN agencies government runners, private sectors, local NGOs, International NGOs, local community and the displaced community. The aim of UNHCR emergency shelters response it to reduce protection to prevent loss of life, in the following issues:

- Preparedness for emergency
- Leadership in emergency shelters
- Delivery
- Technical capacity
- Partnership
- Coordinance
- Shelter solution

UNHCR has capacity to respond to emergency needs of the affected population who were left nothing, UNHCR has capacity to building emergency and providing shelter to displaced persons, in word refugees and internally displaced persons. UNHCR has more than six decades of helping the world uprooted people.

Capacity Building

As a core activity in strengthening 'capacity building under the international protection no. 10: claims to refugees' status within the context of Article 1A(2) of 1951 convention and the 1967 protocol relating to the situation of refugees of 3 December 2013, seeks to help in the protection of refugees though livelihood programmes by UNHCR, develop the capacity to strengthen and to make people self-sufficient in their places.

Capacity building activities are basically ensured under the law of protection for handling refugees' issues, care and self-reliance but it cannot be generated without donor agencies, humanitarian assistance, civil society, NGOs and with the refugees itself.

Due to lack of income and means to earn a living, Bhutanese refugees are entirely dependent on relief agencies as they are not permitted by the host government to engage in any paid work or to produce goods for sale and work outside the camps. So, they work within confines of fields (Women's Refugee Commission, 2006). Over time, they have developed alternative livelihood strategies, such as:

- They produce crops in the camps area and livestock activities.
- Receive incentives from aid agencies and remittance from family members abroad.
- Run a small-scale business in various sectors including small shops, drug stores, the sale of telephone cards, small restaurants and bars, transport of goods and persons, repair services (bicycles, cars and radios), hairdressing, money exchange, phone services, security and language tutoring or interpreting.
- Their production activities include carpentry and furniture making blacksmithing and welding, production of bricks and soap, baking and food processing and production of baskets, leatherwear, textiles and clothes.
- They work with humanitarian agencies or incentive work where formal employment is not allowed which provides a share of refugees with a regular income.
- They work in the position as teachers, nurses, community workers, office staff, cleaners, cooks and gardeners (Bruijn, 2009).

Sometimes refugees do adopt negative coping strategies when none of the alternatives provides structural relief or when households or individuals are faced with immediate crises. These strategies include selling off vital assets such as domestic items, clothes and blankets or part of the food rations, or reducing food intake and negotiating loans that cannot be repaid. Hence, they are forced to indulge in crime and illegal activities, such as fraud (e.g., receiving cash and material benefits for repatriation and then returning for re-registration) and theft (crops, cattle and other assets), or to selling sexual services and trafficking (Refugee Watch Online, 2007). Similarly, camps situated in areas are prone to violence and instability which are not favourable to establish productive and structural ways to earn a living. With the passage of time, the support system in the camps has come under increasing strains because of 'donor fatigue' which cuts in the provision of essential services, including food, fuel, medical care and shelter materials (Lænkholm, 2007). Again, the standard services extended to every refugee have now been limited to only most vulnerable ones.

Finally, it is evident that the level of development of the country of asylum is an essential factor in determining the well being and status of the refugees as the country's capacity to assist refugees sets a standard for the living conditions.

Self-management skills are provided to vulnerable refugee women under the Bhutanese Refugee Women's Forum operating in both the camps (UNHCR, 2000). It gives training for various sectors in business management; awareness-raising programmes on gender and domestic violence and leadership training, childcare centre, income generation for women and fire prevention are run for Refugees (UNHCR, 2000). Women held more than half of the decision-making positions in the camps, with two women serving as camp secretaries (UNHCR, 2007). Women's groups are established in each of the camps and informal skills training, social awareness and functional literacy classes are provided to women with specific needs. Foundation of Bhutanese Refugee Aiding the Victims of Violence (BRAVVE) was founded to provide training to mentally challenged people, many of whom were tortured in jail, traumatized and disabled. People are provided training in tailoring, weaving, embroidery, shoemaking, typing and computer literacy (WHO, 1999). Practising these skills enabled the mentally challenged individuals to be productive.

Establishment of a credit scheme helped them purchase sewing machines, equipment and set up small businesses. Both UNHCR and WFP provide funding to Caritas for Vocational Training (VT) to youth from refugee communities who have dropped out of high school. WFP supports for the training of medical staff, implemented by the AMDA. Some 40 women of an equal number of women from the refugee population and adjacent host communities participated in an eighteen-month course in midwifery and nursing (UNHCR/WFP, 2012). WFP with LWF and UNHCR as implementing partners supports a home gardening project to supplement the basic needs.

Solutions

According to the refugee-budget of UNHCR for Bhutanese Refugees has been increasing almost annually since the year 2000 such as 2000-USD 5.1 million; 2001-5.3 million; 2002-5.6 million; 2003-5.5 million; 2004-6.9 million; 2005-6.8 million. 2007, 2008 (UNHCR, 2000), instead, believing that return provided the only humane solution to refugee problems, the UNHCR essentially ran long-term programmes in an emergency mode which were damaging to the long-term welfare of refugees stuck in protracted camp situations. They have already spent years in remote and forgotten camps and lack in wage-earning opportunities, self-sufficiency. So, it needs a solution where they can become productive and contribute to their host societies until the refugees are willing or can return home.

Refugees usually return when they consider it is safe to do so when other interests are met. Moreover, the UNHCR is not in the best position to determine when it is best or most appropriate for repatriation. It has remained only as an organization in a more general humanitarian emergency. So, it has compromised its capacity and willingness to provide protection and has put the agency at the mercy of a much broader set of political and strategic calculations. Because UNHCR needs to raise more and more voluntary funds for its operations, obtain access to increasingly volatile internal situations, win the confidence of competing actors and promote compromise solutions, the agency is not well placed to stand up for protection principles regarding refugees (Loescher, 2001). The office also lacks a strong self-identity and remains uncertain about the precise role it should fulfill with the broader framework of international relations.

DURABLE SOLUTIONS PROMOTED BY UNHCR

The UNHCR has outlined three options to residents of a refugee camp of protracted refugee situation (PRS). These are:

- Voluntary return (repatriation) to their home country.
- Local integration in the country of first asylum.
- Resettlement in a third country.

Repatriation

Voluntary return or repatriation to their home country in conditions of safety and dignity is the most desirable outcome for the individual, their society and the international community. Most refugees want to return to their homes when it is safe to do so. Support for reconstruction, re-integrating and reconciliation helps ensure the success of repatriation as a durable solution. Regarding the local integration of Bhutanese refugees, though it may appear as a solution to the problem, it will legitimize the state of Bhutan to denationalise its population, in the long run 'it could encourage more displacements' (Chetri, 1997). Refugees insist they won't go back to Bhutan. But they want to back to their land and houses and with some assurance of safety. They would like the office of the UNHCR together with that of the UNHCR to be involved. 'We're not asking for the sky,' says Ratan Gazmere of the Association of Human Rights Activists, based in Nepal. These conditions are unlikely to be met, however. As Bhutanese refugees were forced to leave their homes, land and properties in Bhutan large numbers of houses and land left by the refugees in southern Bhutan have been confiscated by the government and have been used to relocate people from other parts of Bhutan or for government purposes (COHRE, 2008). So, it would be difficult to relocate them in the kingdom of Bhutan.

However, in August 2005 the United Nations Principles on Housing and property restitution for refugees and displaced persons were adopted, 'Pinheiro principles' (COHRE, 2008). These principals provide clear guidelines to make it possible for the Bhutanese refugees to return home. Such possibility applies to all refugees irrespective of which option repatriation, local integrating or third country resettlement, the Bhutanese refugees choose. Most importantly, making repatriation possible, the Bhutanese governments should recognize that the Bhutanese refugees have a right to return. All refugees have the right to go back voluntarily to their former homes, lands or places where they used to live, in safety and dignity. That mean that persons displaced against their will must be allowed to return to their former homes and lands, if and whenever they wish to do so.

Local Integration

Local integration in the country of first asylum is the second option suggested by UNHCR when voluntary repatriation is not possible. It is so because the country of first asylum is usually in the same region to refugee's home country and cultural ties can make the integration process more accessible. In the case of Bhutanese refugees, their first logically, the country for asylum is India, but they have their camps and livelihood in Nepal. Local integration is the process in which refuges settle permanently in the host country (Jacobsen, 2001). However, due to political reasons, regional integration in Nepal has not the preferred solution.

The first obstacle is that Bhutanese refugees are perceived as a temporary inconvenience to the host country because they rely heavily on government and international assistance. It creates the sentiment that if locally integrated refugees are not able to sustain themselves without outside assistance that was available in the camps, they will consequently become a permanent burden to the host country.

Second, refugees lack of belonging to the host country due to discrimination. These are great obstacles in the way of local integrations, who often prefer to return to their home country as soon as they deem it safe or live in the hope of being resettled in a third country.

Third, for local integration to take place, it is fundamental to have the participation and willingness of the host government. Preliminary conditions that need to exist before local integration can take place include the involvement and cooperation of the host government.

Resettlement in a 'Third Country'

Resettlement in a third country is used to protect refugees whose life, liberty, safety, health or fundamental human rights are at risk in their country of asylum. It is promoted by UNHCR where returning to their home country, or local integration may not be suitable or as part of a responsibility sharing arrangement. Due to protracted situations resettlement has become a key element in the system of refugee protection. In TCR, refugees are transferred from the country in which they found refuge to another country which agrees to welcome them. The UNHCR generally gives priority to individuals with a high protection need, as well as women and highly vulnerable families. This kind of resettlement is usually recommended for populations that are victims of protracted situations and when neither repatriation nor local integration seems possible.

The effective implantation to a third country presents numerous challenges. First, it depends on refugees to integrate into the new country. They must be able to adapt themselves to the life, culture and socio-economic structures in the host country. It implies that refugees need to take on a wage-earning activity having a minimum level of education that is necessary. But in Bhutanese refugees' situation, they have a language barrier to integrate.

Protection

These are violence that are directed against a person on the basis of their gender or sex. It includes acts that inflict physical, mental, or sexual harm or suffering, threats of such acts, coercion and other deprivations of liberty. Examples of gender-based violence are sexual violence, domestic violence, emotional and psychological abuse, trafficking, forced prostitution, sexual exploitation, sexual harassment and harmful traditional practices, e.g. Female genital mutilation, or widow cleansing. The women's commission for women and children defines the term 'gender-based violence' as, physical, sexual, psychological and economic or socio-cultural attacks by strangers, by family members, by armies and police forces, even by peacekeepers. It includes harassments, sexual exploitation and trafficking (UNHCR, 2001). Though GBV can occur to anyone, i.e. male or female, young or old it disproportionately affects women and girls.

Similarly GBV is unique to refugee situations. Human rights watch examines the uneven response of UNHCR and the government of Nepal to GBV in refugee camps in Nepal despite reforms by UNHCR though one can experience some positive aspects in the camps but cannot be confirmed. Due to unemployment people are not able to carry their socio-economic roles and increase of family tensions. This results in the subsequent rise in the use of alcohol by men within the refugees' community and leads to aggressive behaviour towards women and results in SGBV.

It has been argued that gender relations in refugees camp are influenced by traditional ideologies and are shaped by memories of home as a domestic sphere of the patriarchal family. And it is well known that the Bhutanese refugees' culture is a patriarchal dominant. So, within the camps, there is a tradition where women bound to remain within the periphery of household activities and dependent on men in the process of getting aid. They have a lower and subordinate position and are subjected to various forms of violence and discrimination. In the case of women the main causes of being the victim are the economic hardship and lack of education and skills. Many women are forced to cross the border to seek better and secure lives are involved in sex businesses workplace harassment and abuse, vulnerability, personal safety and security question of sustainability of income and assistance have become a daily challenge to human right watch reports, SGBV is widespread and have been occurring among Bhutanese refugees in many forms including domestic violence, e.g. fighting and sexual assault, harassment, trafficking, enforced prostitution and sexual violence. Also in the camps, cases of polygamy and child marriage against refugee women, including refugee girls, were reported. Perpetrators of this violence against women include not only partners but also humanitarian aid workers, sexual harassment com-mitted by Nepalese government officers, most of the teachers, working for NGOs implementing partners. In 2001, an investigation team from the inspector general's office investigated all camps with a particular focus on the incidents of SGBV against female refugees, including children. The team reported a total of 47 cases in which ten refugee teachers; one refugee health worker, one sanitation volunteer and two Nepali government officials were said to have been addressed (UNHCR, 2001).

According to WCRWC, incidents of gender-based violence in camps include an attack on women and girls collecting firewood located near to forests (UNHCR, 2006). These are again the results due to a shortage in kerosene supply and which have necessitated firewood collection mainly by those refugees without having sufficient means (UNHCR, 2006). Despite all limitations and discrimination, some definite improvement and steps towards empowerment are seen. Women hence are managing to have a good education and raising their awareness. In recent years, they have found along with colleague 'Voice for change', only independent women's organization in the camps which advocates for women's rights. It has given women the opportunity to express themselves and defend themselves against violence. It has also helped to raise women's voices and has created a platform for discussion, for sharing experiences and finding solutions. Its primary objective is to highlight the issues, inform women and help them understand their problems. Their advocacy activities have been sustained by local NGOs such as TEW Nepal, by the Global Fund for Women and INGO. Hence it can be said that the external influences of international aid workers have made changes through programmes which include training, information support services and for local women and public education events. Gender-based violence cases have been given the priority in the third country resettlement.

The OHCHR plays a role in monitoring and investigating human rights abuses, including those directed against women and girls. UNICEF, for its part, responds to the specific needs of refugee. NGOs are also crucial protection sectors. They partner with UN agencies and work on their own to implement programmes to prevent and respond to SGBV in refugee settings.

Health and Sanitation

The refugee experiences have significant impact on health due to several adverse situations in their country of origin and during their flight and still in the life in exile. The following are some of the deprivation, civil unrest separation and loss of family and friends, imprisonment, threat, beatings, torture and rape, over-crowded, poor hygiene and undernutrition, inadequate health care due to the distraction of infrastructure, disruption in preventive services and limited health services while fleeing or in exile (Mitchell, 2003). Some of the common health problems seen among Bhutanese refugees are: Psychological; issues including PTSD, anxiety or depression; due to torture, poor health as a result of poor nutrition, diet, lack of fluoridated water, infectious diseases including ongoing risks from tuberculosis and chronic intestinal parasites, underimmunization, under-managed chronic condition such as hypertension, diabetes and chronic pain and lastly, delayed growth and development in children including deficits in hearing and speech (Mitchell, 2003).

In 2010, due to all allegation of the disproportionately high number of suicides among refugees resettled in the US, in January 2011, the IOM in coordination with UNHCR conducted a three-week assessment on psychosocial well-being and suicide risk factors among refugees in Nepal and the ones resettled in the US. Results for this confirm that the number of suicides among refugees in Nepal camp is disproportionately high and the rate among refugees resettled in the US is even higher (Schininà, Sharma, Gorbacheva & Mishra, 2011). Besides, health programmes and awareness are provided under UNHCR among refugee camps mainly on subjects related to health education, including HIV/AIDS prevention, family planning, inoculations, mother and child health projects, ambulance services and maintenance of health facilities (UNHCR,

2008) although, different health and nutrition programme are implemented in the camps. In 2007, the Women's Refugee Commission launched a major research project to assess the situation for those living with disabilities among displaced and conflict-affected populations. Because people living with disabilities may be left behind during flight, or may not survive the journey, they are often not identified or counted in registration or data collection exercises; they are excluded from or unable to access mainstream assistance programmes and forgotten when specialized services are set up.

The WRC was particularly concerned about discrimination by their gender, age and social status, as well as their disability. Some positive examples of the refugee community outreach health programmes for persons with a disability were found in the refugee camps (Reilly, 2007). Regarding the availability of inclusive education for children with disability in refugee camps in Nepal, there was successful early childhood intervention programmes to identify children with disability and help them integrate into mainstream schools (Reilly, 2007).

Health status of refugee is a complex issue as it is related to numerous factors, such as food supply, water and sanitation, shelter, education, environmental factors, health services, etc. So to understand the issue, one needs to have a comprehensive approach. Primarily, refugee camps are too compact and overcrowded, which may result in easy spread or transmission of infectious disease. The provision of adequate sanitation services is crucial to prevent communicable diseases and epidemics while ensuring good health and dignity. This part of the study includes human excreta disposal, waste water disposal, solid wasted and clinical waste management and hygiene promotion as a part of sanitation. The collection and disposal of waste should not endanger the individuals and the community. In Nepal, sanitation facilities are designed with women's needs in mind and to avoid vulnerability to SGBV. All families have designated restroom that is shared with one other family and this has provided adequate sanitation coverage. On critically reviewing the sanitation situation in the refugee camps, camps are adequately planned with adequate infrastructure with the refugee managing most of the relief activities with agency coordination. Solid waste management and vector control were carried out through the construction and repair of latrines spraying in the camps. Camps sanitary conditions remained good; vector-borne diseases were kept at negligible levels (UNHCR, 2004). Restrooms were maintained, garbage was collected and clean-up and campaigns conducted regularly within the camps. Construction materials were provided to refugee families to replace over 2,400 latrine roofs and sanitation volunteers helped refugee families to shift close to 3,400 latrine pits. In 2004, a joint solid waste collection, transportation and disposal project was implemented for refugees and host community residents in Beldangi and Sanischari camps (UNHCR, 2004). Shapkota Prajapati describing the Water Supply and Sanitation of Refugee Camp in Nepal writes, 'Excreta disposal, solid waste management and wastewater disposal have been found satisfactory and people's participation is an example to be followed elsewhere' (Kota & Lee, 2006). UNHCR/WFP Joint Assessment Mission Report founded that in general the activities related to water supply and sanitation were functioning well. Periodic clean-up campaigns are organized and garbage is disposed at proper site safe for both the refugee and local population (UNHCR, 2008).

Food and Nutrition Status among Refugees

In the refugee camp situation like in Nepal, people are entirely dependent on humanitarian assistance and food aid. This is primarily because of the host country's policies which restrict income-generation and agricultural activities of refugees. Hence, they entirely depend in the WFP assistance for food which ensures access to adequate quality of food to support life and preserve dignity of refugees. It has the responsibility for the management of the entire food delivery and distribution whereas UNHCR supplements the rations of people with specific needs such as dried skimmed milk was provided to malnourished refugee children. Safe drinking and domestic water supply are provided in all camps.

TABLE 7.2: FOOD AND NUTRITION STATUS AMONG REFUGEES

Camp	*Population*	*General Ration Beneficiaries*
Beldangi	37,311	36,679
Sanischari	11,279	10,993
TOTAL	48,590	47,672

Source: UNHCR/WFP Joint Assessment Mission Report (2008-2012) (UNHCR/WFP, 2012).

Food rations are distributed every two weeks to each household in proportion to the number of members in the family. Refugees receive 'food baskets' containing rice, lentils, vegetable oil, sugar, salt, wheat soya blend and some vegetables. In addition, the food ration reflects cultural and dietary preference of refugees (UNHCR/ WFP, 2012). UNHCR maintains a standard of below 2,100 kilocalories for food and nutrition as average number of kilocalories per person per day.

TABLE 7.3: FOOD AND NUTRITION STATUS AMONG REFUGEES

Commodity	*General rations (grams/persons/day)*
Rice (polished white)	400
Pulses (yellow split peas)	60
Vegetable Oil/Palmolian Oil (Vitamin A fortified)	25
Super cereals (Wheat soya Blend with Sugar)	35
Sugar	20
Salt	7.5

Source: UNHCR/WFP Joint Assessment Mission Report (2008-12) (UNHCR/ WFP, 2012).

UNHCR recommended that each refugee receive more than 2,100 calories per day, but often camps fall short of this standard. Even if a refugee receives the recommended number of calories per day, caloric intake is further reduced as refugees tend to sell food rations for other non-food goods. Moreover, it is not only the quality of food that is insufficient, but lack of food variety, fruits and vegetables also causes many refugees to suffer from deficiencies in essential vitamins and minerals leading to variety of diseases. However, a market in the camps and gardening provides refugee families with fresh vegetables, condiments and other items to supplement their diets. But the lack of farmland restricts families from growing more vegetables. To minimize this deficiency among refugee children, all adolescent girls received iron tablets and all children attending school received deworming tablets (UNHCR/WFP, 2012). Hence over the year the provision of vegetable provided has been reduced, it forced people to earn income and buy food to supplement their ration and to ensure that their diet remains healthy. Similarly, a nutrition and food security strategic plan has been developed in coordination with operational partners to provide improved the nutrition situation among refugees in Nepal (UNHCR/WFP, 2012).

WFP, UNHCR, the RCU and LWF participate in the committee and together agree who would be added or removed from distribution and registration lists in the camp. The committee review the list of departure to third country and adjust the food distribution lists accordingly whereas Asian Medical Doctor's Association (AMDA) is responsible for post distribution food basket monitoring (UNHCR/WFP, 2012). Lastly, as noted above, all the overall food and nutritional status of the refugees is satisfactory.

UNHCR is responsible through its partners for the distribution of non-food items. To prevent environmental degradation particularly from the forest and mainly the increasing fuel prices the regular supply of kerosene to the camps ceased in December 2005. It was used as the most viable source of fuel for cooking in the camps since 1992. Kerosene, replaced by briquettes has hugely impacted on the refugees as briquettes burn slowly, produces a foul smoke and cannot be used as lighting fuel. It prevents children from studying after dark.

REFUGEE WELFARE

Nepal is not signatory in the 1951 refugee convention or the 1967 protocol. Refugees are considered foreigners and are not allowed to engage in economic activities or own any kind of property (UNHCR/WFP, 2012).

Since 2008, the most significant change in refugee welfare has been seen in remittance from abroad. Many shops advertising money transfers are located outside of the camp. Although, these services are utilized by beneficiaries of both the communities. For increment of their diet they use to purchase food and non-food items. They are also used to pay off debts, to provide loans to others, or set aside for contingencies such as fire (UNHCR/WFP, 2012).

Some refugees have started business or open shop in the camp. Other have used the fund to pursue their skill training or advance education. The standard of living has increased in the camp population; it is clearly visible to mission members in the electricity supply, TV sets and satellite dish antenna (UNHCR/WFP, 2012).

Skill and Vocational Training

Skill trainings are very useful for the refugees so that they can be considered for the resettlement. Here the list of skills includes computer software and hardware, finance, driving, tailoring, housekeeping, hair dressing, beautification, masonry, carpentry, plumbing, electric wiring and repair of radios/electric equipment (UNHCR/WFP, 2012). Although, some refugees have complained that in many courses they were not eligible for selected courses as they did not qualify the eligibility criteria (UNHCR/WFP, 2012).

With the support of WFP, the Bhutanese Refugee Women's Forum (BRWF) implements a Loan Scheme. Single women, large families, families without extra support are the beneficiaries. Apart from that at the large scale most of the refugees hesitate to take advantage of the scheme (UNHCR/WFP, 2012).

UNHCR has invested in extension in capacity building, Health workers by means of training, orientation and regular monitoring and supervision by the staff, but as per resettlement health workers poses a serious challenge to the goal of maintaining the quality of health services to the camp population (UNHCR/WFP, 2012).

Funding

UNHCR presented a global needs-based budget of US$ 3,924 million for 2013, for approval to its executive committee for requirement in October 2012. In emergency needs the fund reaches a precedent level of US$ 5,335 million in total requirement by the end of December 2013. However, the funds available could cover only 60 per cent, leaving many of the needs of people a concern to UNHCR (UNHCR, 2012). It should be noted that in this report all expenditure has been modified cash basis, where (UNHCR, 2012) as UNHCR's financial statements are prepared in accordance with International Public Sector Accounting Standards (IPSAS).

UNHCR's financial requirement in Nepal has been increasing with the reduction of refugee population in the camps, with the aim of improving refugee's living standard. In comparison of 2012 Nepal's overall budget requirement slightly decreased. While hosting refugee community will prioritize the resettlement programme with UNHCR (UNHCR, 2013).

Other urban community will continue, undertaking advocacy to ensure the new constitution provision with regards to citizen provision. Short falls consequences in Fund:

- It will hurt the opportunity of skills and resettlement of the refugees.
- Refugees will suffer in reduction of education in schools, vocational trainings and lack of resources for replacement.
- They drastically suffer in basic services and non-food items with supply of fuel and constructions of semi-permanent camps for vulnerable.
- Issues like SGBV would be negatively affected (UNHCR, 2013).

Comparative Planning Figures for Nepal by UNHCR, 2007 and December 2013.

CONCLUSION

The efforts of the UNHCR for well being of the Bhutanese refugees in Nepal, who moved from Bhutan in 1990, have been tremendous, meanwhile they have been constrained by the situation rising on ground. Having been thrown away from their homes and motherland, livelihood and for individual development of the refugees, are critically disrupted and they have been largely

TABLE 7.4: COMPARATIVE PLANNING FIGURES FOR NEPAL BY UNHCR, 2007 AND DECEMBER 2013

Type of Populaton	*Origin*	*Total*	*Of whom assist by UNHCR*	*% of female*	*% of under 18*
Refugees	Bhutan	107,800	107,800	49	34
	Tibetans	20,200	–	48	–
	Various	220	220	-	–
Refugee-like situations	Bhutan	2,500	–	49	34
Asylum seekers	Bhutan	1,600	–	42	31
	Various	80	80	–	–
IDPs		50,000	50,000	–	–
Returnees (IDPs)		50,000	50,000	–	–
Stateless		800,000	–	–	–
Other of concern	Various	140	130	–	–
TOTAL		1,032,540	208,230		

Source: UNHCR Global Report 2007 (UNHCR, 2007).

TABLE 7.5: PERSONS OF CONCERN 2018

Type of Populaton	*Origin*	*January 2018*		*December 2018*	
		Total in country	*Of whom assisted by UNHCR*	*Total in country*	*Of whom assisted by UNHCR*
Refugees	Bhutan	32,338	39,810	28,190	28,190
	Tibetans	15,000	–	15,000	–
	Various	280	280	280	280
Persons in Refugee-like situations	Bhutan	1,890	–	1,890	–
Asylum seekers	Various	20	20	30	30
IDPs	Nepal	50,000	–	50,000	–
Stateless people	Stateless	*	*	*	*
Other of concern		660	250	660	250
TOTAL		100,188	40,360	96,050	28,750

Source: UNHCR Global Appeal Report Update 2018.

dependent on humanitarians' assistance and policies and local conditions in the host country. It is commendable that the UNHCR through its programmes namely basic needs and assistance, capacity building, has attempted to provide durable solutions like repatriation and their local integration. These solutions have eased the settlement, but refugees still face the tough times in fulfilling their wish to go back to Bhutan and settle on their erstwhile homeland, especially the land where their ancestors had settled centuries ago which they are denied now. It is notable that a third country resettlement of the refugees around the globe requires protection, health and sanitation, food and nutrition and other welfare programmes and in the case of the Bhutanese refuges, efforts of the UNHCR and other NGOs and International NGOs can neither be denied nor be ignored. Among the many of the UNHCR led programmes, the most effective contribution has been the financial assistance provided by the UNHCR. In Nepal, to facilitate refugees' integration into the local context and to avoid resentment among the locals surrounding refugee camps, residents for certain assistance are targeted, such as, for example in health care, education, water and food supply. Community-based projects in the camps has been often more efficient in providing services. Implementing partners are working in closer cooperation with the refugees themselves. Without adequate and timely protection mechanisms and proper community-support, the protection and assistance to these vulnerable sections would be more critical.

Also, it is not the issue of the third country settlement and improving the life quality, the other aspect of the Bhutanese refugees in past three decades has revolved around the question of the life with dignity and access to civil, political, economic and educational rights that have been guaranteed under the universal declaration of the human rights, convention on civil and political rights, followed by the convention of the economic rights. While the refugees hold no political rights, allowing them to participate in the process of the governance, they are left to rely on the goodwill and efforts of the agencies like local NGOs and the international agencies like UNHCR. Further, since the ousting of the Nepali-speaking Bhutanese refugees to a third country, their situation has remained static rather turning into complete change. Also, a third country settlement of the refugees does not guarantee the change into their lives, it only guarantees shelter and food with other limited options for education and skill development. With efforts made at the non-governmental level, Nepal has hosted them for three decades now, but the local resistance in the host country is wide open. The Maoist insurgency in the past decade and unstable political turf in Nepal, options for the refugees in terms of political will to pressurize the government of Bhutan to accept them and even improve their life quality in Nepal remains a challenge. Hence, the political will and government response of the host country is the need of the hour for the wellness and hopes for the repatriation of the refugees in Bhutan in near future.

REFERENCES

Amnesty International (December 1992). *Bhutan: Human Rights Violations Against the Nepali-Speaking Population in the South.* Retrieved 26 March 2018 from Amnesty International https://www.amnesty.org/download/Documents/192000/asa140041992en.pdf

Amenesty International (December 1994). *Bhutan: Forced Exile.* Retrieved 25 November 2018, from Amenesty International: https://www.amnesty.org/download/Documents/184000/asa140041994en.pdf

Bhutan Population (18 December 2018). Retrieved from Worldometers: http://www.worldometers.info/world-population/bhutan-population/

Bruijn, B.D. (July 2009). *Human Development Research Paper 2009/25, The Living Conditions and Well-being of Refugees.* Retrieved 11 June 2018 from UNDP: http://hdr.undp.org/sites/default/files/hdrp_2009_25.pdf

Chetri, R. (1997). *Bhutanese Lhotshampas: Victims of Ethinic Cleansing.* In T. K. Bose and R. Manchanda, *State, Citizens and Outsiders: The Uprooted People of South Asia* (p. 265). Kathmandu: South Asia Forum.

COHRE (March 2008). *Hoping to Return Home Housing, Land and Property Restitution Rights for Bhutanese Refugees and Displaced Persons.* Retrieved 12 November 2018 from Centre on Housing Rights and Evictions (COHRE): http://www.chs.ubc.ca/archives/files/Hoping%20to%20Return%20 Home%20Housing, %20land%20and%2 0property%

20 restitution%20rights%20for%20Bhutanese%20Refuges% 20 and%20displaced% 20persons.pdf

Frelick, B. (30 March 2011). *For Bhutan's Refugees, There's No Place Like Home.* Retrieved 25 December 2015, from Human Rights Watch: https:// www.hrw.org/news/2011/03/30/bhutans-refugees-theres-no-place-home

Human Rights Watch (May 2007). *Last Hope: The Need for Durable Solutions for Bhutanese Refugees in Nepal and India.* London: MacMillan Press with UNRISD. Retrieved from Human Rights Watch.

Hutt, M. (2003). *Unbecoming Citizens: Culture, Nationhood and the Fight of Refugess from Bhutan.*New Delhi: Oxford University Press.

—— (2005). The Bhutanese Refugees: Between Verification, Repatriation and Royal Realpolitic. *Peace and Democracy in South Asia*, 45.

Jacobsen, K. (2001). *The Forgotten Solution: Local Integration for Refugees in Developing Countries 96 Packard Avenue Medford, 02155.* Working Paper, Center Tufts University, Fletcher School of Law & Diplomacy and Feinstein International Famine, Massachusetts . Retrieved 23 March 2018, from https://www.unhcr.org/research/working/3b7d24059/forgotten-solution-local-integration-refugees-developing-countries-karen.html

Kharat, R. (2007). *Indo-Bhutan Relations: Strategic Perspective.* In K. Warikoo, *Himalayan Frontier of India* (pp. 155-6). New York: Routledge.

Kota, P. and Lee, S.-H. (October-December 2006). *Water Supply and Sanitation: A Case Study of Timai Bhutanese Refugee Camp in Nepal. Thammasat lnt, 2*(4), 65-7.

Lænkholm, C. (2 December 2007). Resettlement for Bhutanese Refugees. *Forced Migration Review* (29).

Loescher, G. (Spring 2001). The UNHCR and World Politics: State Interests vs. Institutional Autonomy. *The International Migration Review, 35*(01), pp. 36-56.

MHA, GoB (1958). *The Nationality Law of Bhutan, 1958.* Retrieved 11 December 2018, from National Council of Bhutan: http://www. nationalcouncil.bt/assets/uploads/docs/acts/2017/Nationality-law-of-Bhutan-1958_Eng.pdf

Mitchell, S. (2003). *Health Care for Refugees.* Asia Pacific Family Medicine. Retrieved 13 November 2018 from https://onlinelibrary.wiley.com/doi/ epdf/10.1046/j.1444-1683.2003.00063.x

Refugee Watch Online (22 May 2007). *Bhutanese Refugees: Pawn in the Hands of Governments and Politicians?* Retrieved 25 October 2018, from Refugee Watch online: http://refugeewatchonline.blogspot.com/2007/05/ bhutanese-refugees-pawn-in-hands-of.html

Reilly, R. (2007). Disabilities among refugees and conflict-affected populations. *Forced Migration Review*(35), pp. 8-10.

Rose, E.L. (1977). *The Politics of Bhutan.* Ithaka: Cornell University.

Schininà, G., Sharma, S., Gorbacheva, O., & Mishra, A. (2011). *Who am I?: Assessment of psychosocial needs and suicide risk factors among Bhutanese refugees in Nepal and after the third country resettlement.* Geneva: Migration Health Research Portall. Retrieved 20 May 2017, from https://migrationhealthresearch.iom.int/who-am-i-assessment-psychosocial-needs-and-suicide-risk-factors-among-bhutanese-refugees-nepal-and

UNHCR (2000). *Nepal: Mid-Year Report 2000.* Retrieved from UNHCR: https://www.unhcr.org/afr/3e6f1b770.pdf

—— (1 January 2000). *The State of The World's Refugees 2000: Fifty Years of Humanitarian Action.* Retrieved 23 March 2016, from UNHCR: https://www.unhcr.org/publications/sowr/4a4c754a9/state-worlds-refugees-2000-fifty-years-humanitarian-action.html

—— (2001). *Global Report.* Retrieved 1 April 2018, from UNHCR: https://www.unhcr.org/research/working/3b7d24059/forgotten-solution-local-integration-refugees-developing-countries-karen.html

—— (2004). *Global Report: Nepal.* UNHCR. Retrieved 11 December 2017, from https://www.unhcr.org/publications/fundraising/42ad4da50/unhcr-global-report-2004-nepal.html

—— (2006). *Women's Commission For Refugee Women and Children.* Retrieved 19 April 2018, from Library of Congress: https://www.loc.gov/item/lcwa00089057/

—— (2007). *Global Report.* Retrieved 12 November 2018, from unhcr: https://www.unhcr.org/gr07/

—— (2008). *Global Report: Partnerships.* Retrieved 19 May 2018, from UNHCR: https://www.unhcr.org/4a2d1a012.pdf

—— (2010). *Global Trends 2010.* Retrieved 25 December 2017, from UNHCR: https://www.unhcr.org/statistics/country/4dfa11499/unhcr-global-trends-2010.html

—— (2012). *Displacement: The New 21st Century Challenge/Global Trends 2012.* Retrieved 11 May 2018, from UNHCR: https://www.unhcr.org/statistics/country/51bacb0f9/unhcr-global-trends-2012.html

—— (2013). *Global Appeal Update.* UNHCR. Retrieved 11 December 2018, from https://www.unhcr.org/ga13/index.xml

—— (2013). *Global Report.* Retrieved 12 January 2016, from UNHCR: https://www.unhcr.org/gr13/index.xml

—— (1 May 2013). *Refugee resettlement referral from Nepal reaches six-figure mark.* Retrieved 23 November 2018, from UNHCR: https://

www.unrefugees.org/news/refugee-resettlement-referral-from-nepal-reaches-six-figure-mark/

—— (2018). *Resettlement.* Retrieved 19 December 2018, from UNHCR: https://www.unhcr.org/resettlement.html

UNHCR/WFP (2012). *Joint Assessment Mission Report Assistance to the Refugees from Bhutan in Nepal (18 June–8 July 2012).* Retrieved 26 June 2018, from World Food Programme: https://documents.wfp.org/stellent/groups/public/documents/ena/wfp193224.pdf?iframe

WHO (1999). *Making a Difference.* Retrieved 13 July 2018, from World Health Organisation: https://www.who.int/whr/1999/en/whr99_en.pdf?ua=1

Women's Refugee Commission (2006). *Beyond Firewood: Fuel Alternatives and Protection Strategies for Displaced Women and Girls.* WRC. Retrieved 30 October 2016, from https://www.womensrefugeecommission.org/firewood/resources/165-beyond-firewood-fuel-alternatives-and-protection-strategies-for-displaced-women-and-girls

CHAPTER 8

China's Role in South Asia

SUJIT KUMAR DATTA and
TUMPA PAUL

INTRODUCTION

The rising power China has implications for the international system as it is challenging the global structure, but in terms of security its implications are more visible at the regional level. China is the biggest neighbour of all the South Asian countries. The country has age-old, multidimensional, deep-rooted and good relations with all the member states of the regional organization SAARC. Chinese soft power has reached the grassroots in South Asian region. China's role in this region is multidimensional and increasing day by day. For China, getting the global power status, South Asian region plays a vital role and its escalating engagement in political, economic, security and cultural areas with this region is noteworthy. On the other hand, South Asian countries are also very eager to build up smooth relationship with the second largest economy of the present world, China. In China's foreign policy, this region is in priority list and on the other side South Asian countries could always play the China card to evade India's influence. Second, India's new South Asia policy with the focus on trade and connectivity has improved regional cooperation since 1991. But China remains an economically more attractive and politically more reliable partner for India's neighbours. Current strategic and economic trends indicate that South Asia's importance in China's national security calculus is likely to increase in the twenty-first century. A Sino-Indian rivalry in southern Asia and the northern Indian Ocean may well be a dominant feature of future Asian geopolitics.

THEORETICAL FRAMEWORK

One of the major changing pattern of Chinese foreign policy is Beijing's changing political, strategic and economic linkages with the developed and the developing world, especially with South Asia. As the father of neorealism Kennth Waltz explained, 'Unipolarity appears as the least stable of international confugurations. Unlikely though it is, a dominat power may behave modernnization, restraint and forbearance.' Even if it does, however weaker state will worry about the future behaviour faced by unbalaced power, states try to increase their own strength or they ally with others to bring the international distribution of power into balance.[1] Tom & Gray (1995) argue that power balancing in Asia is the key to stability, with regionl security regimes not yet likely to be effective.[2] On the other side of the debate liberal and constructivist authors mainly focus on multilateral institutions. Constructivist Alexandar Wendt calls two increasingly accepted basic tanets of constructivism.[3]

In Realism Theory we find that, States therefore prioritize self-interest over collective interest and have to accumulate power in order to survive. Such thinking drives states to attain a favourable balance of power and compete for influence. Balancing can consist of internal balancing building up one's own power, or external balancing while accumulating power through external relations.

In Liberalism Theory we find the friendship and cooperation between states and here in China-South Asia relations these are obvious. China's national role in South Asian region is mostly based on cooperation and understanding. Another important element of Liberalism is freedom and in this relationship, we can see this. Both China and South Asian countries are enjoying their economic, political, cultural, military relations by their own choices not by any external pressure. So, in China-South Asia context realism and liberalism are found most.

HISTORICAL OVERVIEW OF CHINA-SOUTH ASIA

The interactions between China and South Asia could date back to third century but before the mid of twentieth century. During that time there were only cultural and religion interactions between them. Political connection started only after British subcontinent and China recovered independence in late of 1940s. China and South Asia failed to establish comprehensive and mutual benefits relationships before twenty-first century because their economic ties were very weak. China involved in a border conflict with India, the strongest country of South Asian region and on the other hand its friendly relation with Pakistan helped to keep the regional stability. Before twenty-first century, China's foreign policy towards South Asia could be regarded as single dimensional and limited strategy. Only in twenty-first century, the relationship of China and South Asia has been significantly changed and China very positively participated the regional issues for the first time in history. In this consequence, China's South Asia policy was redefined. The relationships between two sides were enlarged, deepened and reorganized. Then many important and positive phenomena have appeared among their relations, also some negative factors emerged and some traditional obstacles remain.[4] During the cold war the intension of China's policy towards South Asia was to secure its western part of territory and avoid the clash with the regional power in South Asia. Furthermore, given India's hegemonic ambitions in South Asia and China's principled opposition to hegemony, the other countries of South Asia have developed good relations with China as a means of restraint on India. However, China is a crucial external partner of South Asia and would play more and more important role on the stage of South Asia. China's diplomatic relations started with the South Asian region since 1950s, when India and Pakistan made this relation with China after very short time of the country's independence. In the twenty-first century China fundamentally has changed its South Asian policy like it has been conducting multidimensional cooperation with all the South Asian countries. Now, the country's aim doesn't limit it in the security issue any longer, China desires to upgrade its relationship with South Asia in all fields. In the beginning of this century, China was greatly involved in this region's issues and clearly showed its intention and capability. At present China's dominant role in South Asia is an important issue in international politics and gradually this national role of China in the areas of politics, economic development, security issues as well as cultural factors is increasing. China is playing a vital role in South Asian region as a very close neighbour and the members of this region are also enjoying a good relationship with this fastest growing economic giant of the world.

CHINA'S ROLE IN SOUTH ASIA

Traditionally, China preferred from the bilateral diplomacy to multi-lateral diplomacy. But, in the recent time, multilateral diplomacy is getting more and more important in Chinese foreign policy. After the great achievement gained by Chinese multilateral diplomacy in South East Asia, China began its attempt to participate in the integration progress of South Asia. Despite being geographically isolated by the Himalayan Mountain range from South Asia, China's role in South Asia is very significant.[5] China shares a common border with five South Asian nations (Afghanistan, India, Pakistan, Nepal and Bhutan) while the other three (Bangladesh, Sri Lanka and Maldives) do not share borders with China. Nepal and Bhutan are situated along the Himalayan range and act as the buffer states between China and India. Though China had a long history of border tensions with India, the cross-border investment and trade continue to take precedence over past security conflicts. China is taking bolder steps to strengthen its position vis-à-vis the United States across Asia in general and South Asia in particular. Chinese involvement in South Asia is mostly focused on the two largest countries of the subcontinent, India and Pakistan. But China's role in other countries of this region is also very remarkable mostly in economic, political, security and cultural areas.

However, with reference to the changing Chinese strategies, Lawrence Saez writes that Chinese policy toward South Asia has shifted subtly and may be experimenting with and pursuing a variety of strategic options like balancing multilateralism with peripheral stability and the pursuance of other security objectives (such as energy security). He further writes that with respect to South Asia, China is pursuing a policy of *reluctant competition* with India; *contingent cooperation* with Pakistan, Bangladesh and Sri Lanka; and *secretive cooptation* with Nepal and Maldives.[6] Pursuing this strategy at regional level, China has joined the South Asian Association of Regional Cooperation (SAARC) in 2005 and has been participating in all SAARC Summits regularly after it got observer's status.

CHINA'S ECONOMIC ROLE IN SOUTH ASIA

China has world's largest population and it is the second largest economy of the world.[7] The country's rise has been treated as one of the greatest events of the last century. It is one of the enigmas of the twenty-first century. Since the adoption of economic reforms and opening-up policy by Deng Xiaoping after 1978, China's economy has been growing at a tremendous rate.[8] China's rise as an economic and trading power has been impressive on many levels.

However, China's economic expansion in South Asian countries is increasing day by day and at present several mega projects connect these countries with China greatly. Though China's economic engagement in this region is later then its political and cultural connection but its economic role in South Asia will be beneficial for the progress and consistency of this region. China's economic growth will give much space to South Asian goods to Chinese markets. China's policy towards this region can be understood through its periphery strategy which focuses on different changing atmosphere and on progress in bordering areas.[9] Due to two reasons, South Asia is important for China. Firstly, China wants stability within state along with peace in bordering areas. Secondly, China's interaction with neighbouring countries is necessary to enhance trade. South Asia has sufficient space for Chinese goods and its economic role was actively observed in this region in 2008 after international economic recession as compared to the past.[10]

From Beijing's perspective, the most important nation in the South Asian region is India. India and China are the two most populous nations on earth. Indeed, India is expected to surpass China sometime in the 2020s. Sino-Indian relations have often been rocky. While the two states enjoyed relatively peaceful relations for the few years after the founding of the People's Republic in 1949, the situation rapidly deteriorated and relations between the two powers have often been frosty. Several factors have played into this, but perhaps the most important factor was and is the border issue between the two countries. The precise demarcation of the border between China and India remains a contentious issue for both sides.[11] Despite this India and China resumed trade in 1978 and in this consequence both countries signed the Most Favoured Nation (MFN) in 1984. In 2008, both countries bilateral trade reached US$ 51.8 billion and has made China as India's largest trading partner in goods replacing the United States of America. But in 2009, because of the world economic downturn, bilateral trade dropped into US$ 43.27 billion and again in 2010 is reached at US$ 61.74 billion. These ups and downs happen as same as in their bilateral trade for last few years also. Commodity-wise, bilateral trade was dominated by reactors, boilers, machinery, electric machinery, sound equipment's, organic chemicals, ores, cotton, etc. China's investment in India is also noteworthy. Economically, China is also a more attractive partner for South Asian countries than India. Though, there are lots of problems in Sino-India bilateral relations but Sino-Indian trade is increasing day by day. In 2017 India export to China $12,495,230,459 and India import from China $71,922,747,817).[12]

The massive Chinese investment in India's neighbourhood in the context of its 'One Belt One Road' (OBOR) Initiative will increase Beijing's influence in South Asia. China has also expanded its trade relations and has surpassed India in some cases. Even in India, China has emerged as a significant economic factor. In the regional context, both countries are cooperating on initiatives like the Bangladesh-China-India-Myanmar (BCIM) economic corridor and China has also promised to make large scale infrastructure investment in India. Despite their bilateral problems and tensions from respective engagement in South Asia, India and China have also increased their collaboration on the global level as well as multilateral perspective like Shanghai Cooperation Organization (SCO), New Development Bank (NDA), Group 20 (G20) and the BRICS (Brazil, Russia, India, China, South Africa).

Even in terms of China's economic engagement, Pakistan remains China's 'biggest market' for its capital investment in infrastructure projects; most of which remain of strategic importance if not directly all part of their defence collaborations. China-Pakistan economic cooperation began in 1979. China has become Pakistan's largest arms supplier and second-largest trading partner. China invests in Pakistan's infrastructural expansion through building of power plants, roads and communication nodes including the Pakistani deepwater port at Gwadar.[13] Both countries are keen on strengthening the economic ties and promised to 'propel' cross-border trade. Pakistan has been granted free trade zone in China. Both countries signed a free trade agreement in 2008 and agreed to build a railway through the Karakoram.[14] At present China's Mega project with Pakistan is China-Pakistan Economic Corridor (CPEC), which will develop Pakistan's economy in a great range.

Chinese Economic role in Bangladesh is increasing in a remarkable way. At present China is the largest trading partner of Bangladesh and both countries are working together to promote the bilateral economic relations and trade cooperation. The People's Republic of China and the People's Republic of Bangladesh officially established diplomatic relations on 4 October 1975. Since then, the friendly relations and cooperation between the two countries have been growing steadily which is termed as 'trusted friendship' or 'all weather friendship'. China is the assistance provider of Bangladesh in the areas of communications, power and energy, infrastructure development, etc. On the other hand, China is the biggest market for Bangladeshi products such as jute, textiles, leather, footwear, tobacco, etc. Chinese investment in Bangladesh is very important for Bangladesh and its rising. Chinese FDI comes to Bangladesh more in textile and China has supported Bangladesh with investments in projects and infrastructure. China's

'One Belt One Road' initiative will increase opportunities for Bangladesh to connect in the economic prosperity. China also considers Bangladesh as an important part and BCIM (Bangladesh-China-India-Myanmar) is very significant for both countries. China's role in the economic development of Bangladesh is noteworthy BCIM can become a way for Bangladesh and India to relate to a pan-Asian market.

In Nepal's development endeavour, China has always been a steady and reliable partner more specifically in the areas of infrastructure and human resources development, education, health and food assistance among others. The first Agreement between China and Nepal on 'Economic Aid' was signed in 1956.[15] In the year 1982 both countries established Inter-Governmental Economic and Trade Committee which focuses on bilateral economic and technical cooperation. China's economic role in Nepal is increasing in the twenty-first century as their trade volume is growing. China is the topmost investor in Nepal and Chinese investment is growing as compared with the past. Regarding development in Nepal, the regular meetings of Inter-Governmental Economic and Trade Committee would be helpful for coordinated overall interactions. The present status of Nepal's trade with China is good under Xi Jinping, as in 2017 the total trade volume between two states was approximately US$ 1.267 billion. Nepal is also connected with China's mega project 'OBOR' initiative, which will create more opportunities for Nepal economic development and will improve the economic tie.

Sri Lanka and China have had historical links that can be traced back from several centuries. China's economic role in Sri Lanka is very significant as China supports in various development projects such as Hambantota Port, Colombo South Harbour, Mattala International Airport[16], etc., and these large-scale investments have the potential to transform economic opportunities, including export development and promote reconciliation through better economic integration within the domestic economy. China also supports in the Norochcholai Power Plant and several Highway, Expressways projects. China is the largest trading partner of Sri Lanka within Asian region and Sri Lanka offered oil exploration block to China and China National Petroleum Corporation (CNPC) started working on it.[17] Both countries are enjoying a very friendly economic environment from both sides. Sri Lanka signed China's 'OBOR' initiative. China's economic rising in the world arena is benefiting Sri Lanka in various aspects.

China's economic role in another South Asian country Bhutan is not a very remarkable one because Bhutan has been a strong ally of India and refrained from establishing relations with China for a long time. Another reason for this gap is the border disputes.[18] But recently Bhutan opened its economy and Chinese companies have been given contract to construct the world's tallest Buddha Statue in Thimpu. Now China is an attractive source of investment and exporting farming and telecommunication equipment, as well as investing in the projects related to health and education services.

The diplomatic relations between China and Maldives were first established in 1972 and since then relations have gradually developed. Bilateral trade between both countries is increasing. China has built Maldives' Ministry of Foreign Affairs building and national Museum. However, China's economic role in this country is increasing and China also provided loans to build the 1,000 housing projects which have served to further expand goodwill and cooperations.[19]

China's economic role in Afghanistan is increasing because US presence in Afghanistan slowly diminishe and China has taken several steps to signal its interest to Kabul as an economic partner. In 2014, for example, China committed 2 billion yuan (327 million) in aid to Afghanistan through 2017, larger than a total of 1.5 billion yuan ($240 million) it had provided in over a decade between 2001 and 2013.[20] China was one of the first countries to invest in mineral extraction in Afghanistan. Afghanistan is poised to benefit from and partner with China through the 'OBOR' initiative. With considerable human talent and financial resources attached to it, the 'OBOR' initiative has the potential to serve as an integral part of the Afghan Government's Infrastructure and Connectivity Development and Private Sector Development National Priority Programs. China is also investing in different development projects in Afghanistan which will improve the county's economic conditions.

CHINA'S GEOPOLITICAL IMPLICATIONS IN SOUTH ASIA

Emphasis on Peace and Stability, China's present political and diplomatic efforts in the region remain focused on easing tensions and maintaining peaceful periphery to ensure environment conducive to her sustained economic development. China remains an economically more attractive and politically more reliable partner for South Asian states then India. Given China's current preoccupations with internal stability, security, modernization and consolidation of territorial limits and strategic space in the Hong Kong-Taiwan-South China Sea sector, it is keen to maintain stable and good relations with the South Asian states.

China and India straddle a common geopolitical space across the Himalayas and South, Southwest and Southeast Asia. This makes for strategic and geopolitical competition. The growth of these two major power centres adjacent to one another would increasingly be a major factor shaping Asia's politico-security environment. Stable relations between these two powers is therefore not only in the interest of their peoples, but also in Asian and global interest. Building the basis for a stable and cooperative relationship is a challenge.

But there are several geopolitical tensions that remain between the two countries such as border disputes, Indian Ocean, etc. The increasing Chinese presence in the Indian Ocean area, therefore, is viewed with much suspicion by India. As Jawaharlal Nehru is reported to have said, 'To be secure on land, we must be supreme at sea'.[21] With a 5,000-mile coastline in the Indian Ocean, Indian strategists have often considered the Indian Ocean as its 'private lake'.[22]

On the other hand, China's relation with Pakistan developed over a long period since 1951, when both countries established diplomatic relations. Pakistan's geopolitical importance to China or any other major powers is very significant as Pakistan located between China, South Asia, on the one hand and Central Asia and West Asia on the other and is at the mouth of the Persian Gulf. Pakistani port of Gwadar is very important for China because of its strategic involvement in the northern areas of Pakistan, Gilgit and Baltistan bordering China. Gwardar provides China the shortest route for its trade with Africa, Middle East and Europe. So, China is working in this port and is matter of concern for India.

Bangladesh is a nation of strategic importance not only to the South Asian region but to the larger geopolitical dynamics of Asia as a whole. Bangladesh enjoys a strategically advantageous location and its geostrategic location is increasingly embedding its relations with China in the international strategic context where the interest of foreign powers set the parameters within which it has to manoeuvre. In terms of its political spin-off, China's growing posture of neutrality in South Asian Affairs has been cited as the most visible outcome that clearly favours New Delhi.[23] Frequent high-level visits of China's officials to South Asian countries and also from those countries to China are making the political tie between China and South Asia stronger and creating many opportunities for both sides.

CHINA'S SECURITY ROLE IN SOUTH ASIA

Chinese objectives in South Asia have been already beyond the traditional security issue. Its linkage with South Asian countries expanded to all fields including economic, communication, energy and the untraditional security cooperation. China's rising military capabilities, especially its nuclear and missile build up, has direct security implications on its neighbours in Asia with whom it has sovereignty disputes, ethnic-related insecurities and tensions and geopolitical rivalries and some of whom Beijing sees as potential threats.[24]

Following its takeover of Tibet, China became an integral part of the Southern Asian geopolitical and strategic environment. It shares borders with Afghanistan, Pakistan (given its occupation of a portion of Jammu & Kashmir), India, Nepal, Bhutan and Myanmar. As neighbouring states, each is affected—some positively and some negatively—by China's military power, posture, strategic thinking and evolving role. China thus shapes in a major way the regional balance of power and security environment. Nearly 90 per cent of China's total arms transfers are targeted at Pakistan, Iran, Myanmar, Bangladesh, Thailand and Sri Lanka, all neighbours of India.[25] China has also developed naval and defense ties with all the Indian Ocean littoral states, dotting the area between the Gulf and Southeast Asia.

On the other hand, land-locked Nepal and Bhutan which have close security relations with India but which would be directly affected by a dominant or a hostile China, by migrations from China as a result of political turmoil in Tibet and by a deterioration in Sino-Indian relations. China's Security role in Afghanistan is also very important. China was a major actor in the Afghan civil war and a key supplier of small arms to the insurgents in the combined effort of United States and Pakistan to force a Soviet withdrawal from the country.

However, non-traditional security issues such as extremism, piracy, managing global commons, etc., are increasingly occupying larger space in strategic considerations. Three powers India, Pakistan and China determine the strategic profile of South Asian security, constitute a security triangle.

CULTURAL EXCHANGES BETWEEN CHINA AND SOUTH ASIA

Cultural exchange or cultural cooperation is a large field of activities and requires analytical attention independently. China-South Asia cultural relations have tremendous potential to bloom and can redefine cultural cooperation to suit the imagination of a new world order. China has adopted a policy of scientific expansion and it will become the most innovative country.

In this consequence, every year Chinese government is offering fellowships and South Asian countries are getting a remarkable portion. In most of the South Asian countries there are Chinese cultural and language centres, Chinese food restaurants, etc. On the other hand, some South Asian states signed agreements on cultural cooperation with China such as Nepal signed it to enhance cultural exchanges. Nepal has been receiving volunteer teachers for Chinese language training and agriculture sector too. Like Nepal, some other countries like Bangladesh, Sri Lanka, Maldives, Pakistan and even with India, China has cultural cooperations. Cultural cooperation between Sri Lanka and China is blossoming in sports, interactions, etc.

PROBLEMS AND FUTURE CHALLENGES OF CHINA-SOUTH ASIA

The relationship between the South Asian countries and China raises several issues related to the old order and the emerging order. In South Asian region, China's role is increasing very significantly but still there are some remarkable challenges which China need to work on for making itself as a regional power compete with India.

Traditional Geo-political Disputes

Judging from the integration achievements gained, the process of integration of South Asia is quite slow and insufficient, sometimes even moves forward two steps but backward one step. It is not economic factor but the long-term rivalry between India and Pakistan hijacked not only the development and expansion of the SAARC, but also the integration process of that region and the other issues including the relations between external players with South Asian countries. The core issue of these two countries traditional geopolitics dispute is Kashmir and since 1998, the nuclear issue has intruded. Even though both sides repeated their good-willing for many times and launched many diplomatic steps to mitigate the situation and promote the bilateral relation, the tension remains and no one could expect it could be relaxed in near future. For any external partners, India and Pakistan dispute is the priority concern when making policy or taking actions towards this region.[26] So, for China this issue is a big challenge in South Asian region.

External Factors Impact

In strategic terms, South Asia was never an important region for the United States of America during the last many years. But now things have changed. Since 1990s, the American South Asia policy transited from Balance Strategy to Beyond Balance Strategy. Alliance between USA and Pakistan, which is against partnership between Russia and India, was renounced by Washington step by step and India became the keystone of USA's South Asia policy. India and USA never addressed any statement or officially admitted their cooperation is confronting China, but in fact, it's very obviously that 'the strongest democracy country' is seeking to ally with 'the most populated democracy country' to balance 'the fastest growing economic entity in the world'. Of course, the cooperation between Washington and New Delhi also covers many other fields, including power security, communication, nonproliferation, etc. But managing China is a very important part.

Trade Disputes

The increasing trade disputes, such as main complains from the local manufactures and anti-dumping investigations came after Chinese increasing commerce links with South Asia in recent years. China enjoyed huge favourable imbalance in all the bilateral trade relations between China and the rest of South Asian countries like Sri Lanka, Bangladesh, Nepal and Maldives. Bhutan is the only exception because there is no direct trade links with China. Although currently the trade conflict remains relative slight and could be controlled, it has already brought a certain negative effect to the relations between China and South Asia. Considering China would preserve the competitive edge in economic arena with South Asia smaller countries even in certain fields with India, it is not expected that the trade disputes would be resolved in short time.

FUTURE OPPORTUNITIES FOR CHINA

Rise of China, decline of America and shift of global power balance from west to the east, or from Europe to Asia or from Atlantic to the Asia-Pacific and Indian Ocean region are common references in most recent discussion on global power balance. China and South Asia between themselves can evolve into a power base for common good. There is only need for connectivity between the two people and civilizations. Greater interaction among the peoples of the two regions will have tremendous impact on exchange of ideas and intellect, of goods and services bringing the fruits of economic prosperity to each other's doorstep. There are several opportunities for China to make its position stronger in South Asian region. China can Balance and Stabilize the Regional Security Environment in South Asia. It is in China's interest to continue pursuing the objective of peace and stability in the region through balance of power and conflict resolution rather than strengthening the hegemonic position of the biggest regional country India. Balance of power in South Asia, does contribute towards China's interests in South East Asia by curtailing India's liberty of action.

On the other hand, China can promote regionalism in the South Asian region. China's entry into the SAARC is likely to reinvigorate the forum and enhance regionalism in South Asia. China, due to its political clout may play an important role in fostering mutual trust, conflict resolution and promoting good neighbourly relations among regional states through SAARC plus one mechanism. Furthermore, China can integrate smaller regional states in economic development: To enhance long-term economic interdependence, South Asian states may be integrated in China's economic development. Moreover, regional anti-terrorism cooperation will be more effective work for the whole South Asian region. United State of America (USA) and North Atlantic Treaty Organization (NATO) seems to be failing stabilizing Afghanistan and curtailing spill-over effects of terrorism to other countries. Here, China can play an important role to stabilize this situation.

Energy is the highest demand for South Asian states. China may be an option for South Asian states to meet their energy needs. China also can help by sharing renewable energies technology like wind and solar power, etc., besides assisting them to explore their untapped mineral and hydropower resources. On the other sides, China can promote soft power image to South Asia for future development. Present level of youth exchange programmes, cultural, sporting and people-to-people interactions may be expanded. Enhanced interaction between universities, think-tanks, academic institutions, mass media and film and television industries are also likely to help China to occupy cognitive space in the region, mitigating the effects of negative propaganda of western media.

CONCLUSION

China's increasing engagement at bilateral and multilateral forums in South Asia has surely increased its leveraging capacity and influence with most of South Asian countries. Especially, given the increasing global interest in South Asian affairs following the nuclear tests by India and Pakistan, China's steady movement towards South Asian multilateralism also seems to be powered by its ambitions to emerge as the next global power. A powerful and prosperous India will also serve as the engine of change for the largest population concentration in the world in South Asia. What South Asia needs is not a containment of China but a realistic engagement strategy that takes the interests of all countries into account. That would involve enmeshing China in trade, investment and multilateral security ties. But it would also entail creating a new South Asian balance and supporting India and other states to secure their interests. Since the end of Cold War, China's policy towards South Asia is undergoing changes both in theory and practice in line with changing global geopolitical environments. Despite China's earnest desire to work in harmony with South Asian nations for common prosperity, mutual benefit and regional peace and stability, the policy faces many future challenges. Considering all things in conclusion it can be said that China's national role in South Asia is increasing remarkably and in the international arena its importance is also increasing.

NOTES

1. Stevenson, H. Howard, *Dolunch or be lunch.* Boston: Harvard Business School Press, 1998.
2. Benjamine Goldsmith, A liberal peace in Asia, *Journal of Peace Research*, 2007, vol. 44, no. 1, p. 7.
3. Alexander Wendt, *Social Theory of International Politics*, Cambridge: Cambridge University Press, 1999, p. 1.
4. China and South Asia: Issues and Future Trends, *International Journal of Liberal Arts and Social Science*, vol. 2, no. 6, August 2014.
5. Zhao Gancheng, 'China India Relations and SAARC', Shanghai Institute for International Studies, Policy Perspectives, *Academic Journal*, June 2012, http://connection.ebscohost.com/c/articles/82457203/china-india-relations-saarc (accessed on 20 June 2018).
6. Lawrence Saez and Crystal Chang, 'China and South Asia: Strategic Implications and Economic Imperatives,' in China, the Developing World and the New Global Dynamic, ed. Lowell Dittmer and George T. Yu, Boulder: Lynne Rienner, 2010, 87.
7. http://worldpopulationreview.com/countries/china-population/ (accessed on 8 December 2018)https://www.weforum.org/agenda/2018/04/the-worlds-biggest-economies-in-2018/ (accessed on 8 December 2018).
8. Zhu Xiaodong, 'Understanding China's Growth: Past, Present and Future,' *Journal of Economic Perspectives*, vol. 26, Fall 2012, pp. 103-24.
9. Ibid., pp. 41-9.
10. Parama Sinha Palit, 'China's Soft Power in South Asia', S. Rajaratnam School of International Studies Singapore, 8 June 2010, pp. 11-12.
11. Christian Wagner, *Asia Pacific Bulletin*, no. 389, 26 July 2017.
12. United Nations Statistic Division https://comtrade.un.org/db/dq BasicQueryResults.aspx?cc=TOTAL&px=HS&r=699&y=2017&p=156&so=9999&rpage=dqBasicQuery&qt=n (accessed on 12 June 2018).
13. 'China, Pakistan joined in bonds of brotherhood'. *People's Daily*. Retrieved 18 January 2014.
14. *The Express Tribune*, APP, 18 December 2010.
15. http://www.mofa.gov.np/en/nepal-china-relations-78.html, Retrieved on 12 December 2013.
16. Sino-South Asian Relations: Economic and Strategic Implications by Akkas Ahamed, Sino-South Asian Relations: Continuity and Change, pp. 241-2.

17. Amal Jayasinghe, 'Sri Lanka eyes South Asian hub with Chinese mega Port'. *Fox News*, 4 August 2013, Retrieved on 2 December 2013.
18. Teshu Sinh, 'China-Bhutan Relations: Implications for Indian Security Analysis, Institute of Peace & Conflict Studies, New Delhi.
19. Sergei De Silva-Ranasinghe, Perth, Australia,opinion, *Jakarta Post*, 2011.
20. Noor Rahman Tahiri, Afghanistan and China Trade Relationship, Oruj University, 2017 available at Online at https://mpra.ub.uni-muenchen.de/82098/ MPRA Paper No. 82098, posted 22 October 2017 07:23 UTC (accessed on 7 December 2018).
21. Vijay Sakhuja, *Asian Maritime Power in 21st Century: Strategic Transactions: India, China and Southeast Asia*, Singapore: Institute of Southeast Asian Studies, 2011, p. 17.
22. Ashley Townshend, 'Sino-Indian Maritime Relations: Managing Mistrust in the Indian Ocean,' Strategic Snapshots, Snapshot 6, *Lowy Institute for International Policy*, December 2010, p. 2.
23. Swaran Singh, *China-South Asia: Issues, Equations, Policies*, New Delhi: Lancer Books, 2003, chapter 14: China's Posture of Neutrality, pp. 343-58.
24. David Shambaugh, 'The Insecurity of Security: The PLA's Evolving Doctrines and Threat Perceptions Towards 2000', *Journal of Northeast Asian Studies*, Spring 1994, pp. 3-25; Also see Ross H. Munro, 'Eaves-dropping on the Chinese Military: Where it Expects War and Where it Doesn't', *Orbis*, vol. 38, no. 3, Summer 1994, p. 355.
25. For arms transfer data, see *SIPRI 1996 Yearbook*; also see the United Nations Arms Register data available since 1992 on seven major categories of weapon systems that form the bulk of the international trade in arms.
26. D.S. Rajan, *China and South Asia—An Indian Perspective*. South Asia Analysis, India, 2011.

REFERENCES

Abraham, F. (2005). *The Rise of China: Prospects for Regional Trade Policy.* Belgium: Centre for Economic Studies.

Chernoff, F. (2000). *The Power of International Relations: Reforging the Link to Foreign Policymaking through Scientific Enquiry.* New York: Routledge.

Cohen, S.P. (2000). *India: Emerging Power.* Washington: Brookings Institution Press.

Dibb, P. (1995). *Towards a New Balance of Power in Asia.* New York: Oxford University Press.

Garver, J.W. (1992). 'China and South Asia'. *The ANNALS of the American Academy of Political and Social Science.* 519(1), 67-85.

Garver, J.W. (2009). *China's South Asian Interests and Policies.*Georgia.

Gupta, B.S. (1972). *The Fulcrum of Asia: Relations among China, India, Pakistan, and the USSR.* New York: Western Publishing Company.

Gupta, R., & Liang, G. (2017). *Elections in Nepal: A Struggle Between the Ballot Box and Buffer.* SADF Comment, (111). Retrieved from http://sadf.eu/new/wp-content/uploads/2017/12/Comment.111.Rishi_Gupta.Gao_Liang.pdf

Hedrick, B.K. (2009). *The Balance of Power in South Asia: The Strategic Interests and Capabilities of India, China and Pakistan.* (Master's thesis, University of Texas). Retrieved from University of Texas repository.

Jiali, M.A. (2003). 'Relations between China and SAARC'. In U. Gautam (ed.), *South Asia and China: Towards Inter-Regional Cooperation* (p. 80). Kathmandu: China Study Centre.

Kapila, S. (2003). Bangladesh China Defense Cooperation Agreements: Strategic Implications. South Asian Analysis Group, Paper No. 582.

Little, D. (2002). South Asia 2020: Future Strategic Balance and Alliances. Conference brief. Studies Institute India.

Nayak, N.R. (2017). China's Growing Military Ties with Nepal. IDSA Comment. Retrieved from https://idsa.in/idsacomments/china-growing-military-ties-with-nepal_nrnayak_310317

Paul, T.V. (2010). South Asia's Weak States: Understanding the Regional Insecurity Predicament. Stanford: Stanford University Press.

Stern, R.W. (2001). Democracy and Dictatorship in South Asia: Dominant Classes and Political Outcomes in India, Pakistan, and Bangladesh. Westport: Greenwood Publishing Group.

Touranbam, M. (2017). Changing India-China-United States Dynamics in South Asia. New Delhi.

Tellis, A.J. (1997). *Stability in South Asia.* RAND Corporation, Arroyo Center.

Terrill, A.W. (2003). Prospect for peace in South Asia. Conference Brief. Washington:Strategic Studies Institute,.

Walt, S.M. (2016). Alliances: Balancing and Bandwagoning. Research Paper. RAND.

Waltz, K.N. (1997). Theory and International Politics. New York: McGraw Hill.

Webber, J.R., Stotts, R., & Wohlers, L. (1997). A National Security Strategy for South Asia. National War College, Washington.

Weber, C. (2005). International Relations Theory: A Critical Introduction. New York: Routledge.

Wei, Y. (2007). A Broader Asia Without China? *Beijing Review,* (38).

CHAPTER 9

Nepal-United States Relations in the Context of Increased Chinese Influence in South Asia

PURNA BAHADUR KARKI

INTRODUCTION

Nepal and the United States established diplomatic relations in 1948. The US has been helping to support Nepal in promoting political stability and economic development and providing humanitarian assistance. Furthermore, the US assists Nepal through bilateral relations for peace and security. Globally, the US and Nepal support each other to achieve both nations' policies and objectives in the international community. Nepal is becoming one of the most important countries to US policy to obtain South Asian security and monitor Chinese and Indian militarism and nuclear security, as well as Pakistani extremism. In contemporary discourse, the presence of the US in South Asia also impacts the global influence of the US.

Historically and in the literature, the Second World War, the Cold War, the post-Cold War era, the aftermath of 9/11, and China's emergence since 2004-5 have all highlighted the importance of South Asia and the Indian Ocean in maintaining and sustaining the superpower image and influence of the US in Asia. When examined, the US policy pursued in South Asia and West Asia during Second World War and the Cold War shows that Sri Lanka supported US interests in countering Russian presence in the region. This indicates how important South Asia is in the US policy and stability programmes, not regional considerations but also for controlling communism and reinforcing but also for controlling communism and reinforcing the US superpower in contemporary Asia.

Additionally, when US policy toward South Asia indirectly was evaluated and observed, through Japan and India, as proxies of the US that implement US policy. Japan has represented the US ever since 9/11 to revitalize and activate policy against global terrorism. The US has sought loyal partners in South Asia and India is a reliable partner just like Japan.

China will collide with the US. It is emerging as an economic powerhouse and is spontaneously threatening US interests, influence and even position in South Asia. China is challenging the superpower image and influence of the US. This first took place in South Asia, where traditional allies of the US, such as Pakistan, Sri Lanka and the Maldives are looking to China for economic and development assistance.

In addition to its political, economic and security interests, China is in search of new markets for investment. China is focusing on giving assistance, such as long-term loans and expertise to South Asian nations, such as Pakistan, Sri Lanka and Nepal and has actively engaged in the region. China proposed the Asian Infrastructure Investment Bank, which will enhance the position of China if it becomes active. This will reduce the influence of the US and Japan. Given these conditions, the US must review its policy program to challenge the Chinese presence.

In its development perspective and policy 'One Belt and One Road' (OBOR), China proposes establishing and creating a network of railways, roads, pipelines and utility grid that would link China and other central Asian nations, which would pave the way for connecting China and the world. This would boost the Chinese involvement in this region, as well as providing a platform for economic cooperation, including policy coordination, trade and financing collaboration and social and cultural cooperation. This would enhance the Chinese initiative towards a leadership position in the world forum, where recently US policy and programmes have worked against the member countries. Also, Trump's policy of 'America First' opens the US to more criticism in international relations, which might be problematic for sustaining a US leadership role in the world forum.

Further, in the future, how China builds its military power against traditional American allies will determine the superpower image of the US in the region. Moreover, recent developments involving regional tension and allies, as well as national internal conflicts, have gone against American interests. In this situation, the American policy programme is important in Asia, where China, North Korea, South Korea, Philippines and Japan are all suffering from internal conflicts involving security and disputes in the South China Sea.

Recently, the media, politicians and academics have debated the leadership change in the US government in the Trump era in both positive and negative ways. Trump's bilateralism may provide more opportunities for the American people and may build stronger bonds with the international community. However, some fear that extreme policies might reduce US global power. But not only it gives the US a clear road to power but also provides security for the US. In this chapter, the following hypotheses are tested:

(i) Trump's bilateralism policy will have *good/bad* implications for stability in Asia.
(ii) Nepal can play an important role as an intermediary between the US and China.

Further, explorations regarding relations between the US and Nepal in the context of China's increased influence in South Asia during the Trump era is done.

METHODOLOGY

This research employed a multifaceted approach to data collection and analysis, with a strong emphasis on qualitative methods. Secondary data were gathered through an extensive literature review and systematic comparison. To gain a comprehensive understanding of contemporary discourse concerning Nepal and the United States, as well as their politico-economic and societal contexts, qualitative aspects of social components were meticulously examined. Additionally, historical analysis was conducted to contextualize these findings within a broader temporal framework.

NEPAL AND INDIA RELATIONS IN THE CONTEXT OF INCREASED CHINESE INFLUENCE IN SOUTH ASIA

Nepal and India have cordial bilateral relations and they share common cultural elements, traditions, and religion. According to the Ministry of Foreign Affairs on Nepal-India relations, it states that the two countries established diplomatic relations on 17 June 1947. In principles of peaceful coexistence, sovereign equality and understanding of each other's aspiration and sensitivities, Nepal and India not only have relations through treaties and agreements between the two countries but also have people-to-people contact and free movements of people between the countries. At the political level, Nepal and India have good relations, with frequent high-level visits by the leaders between the two countries. Recently, for example, Prime Ministers exchanged visits within a short period. This illustrates the importance of India-Nepal relations at the political level.

Looking back to Nepalese leaders' state visits to India, it indicates that almost all Nepali political leaders and Prime Minsters visited India after they assumed office. Reciprocally, an invitation from Nepal's then Prime Minister, Sushil Koirala, led to an official visit to Nepal in August 2014, by the Prime Minister of India, His Excellency Shri Narendra Modi. This was a historic visit by a prime minister of India to Nepal, after 17 years, which reflected the commitment of the newly-formed government in India to enhance India's relations with neighbouring countries (Ministry of Foreign Affair, Nepal, 2017. This indicates the importance of Nepal relations to India after the change of leadership in India in response to China's increasing development assistance and engagement in this region.

In relation to the Prime Minster of India's third visit on Nepal within a four-years' period, Thapa (2018) states, 'India has realized by now that the use of coercive diplomacy severely dented bilateral relations. Therefore, India wants to revamp its image in Nepal and Modi's reciprocal visit within a month of Oli's visit to India signals the urge and necessity to do so'. Also, Bagachi Indrani (2018) states that it is 'to reset ties'. Analysis of the state level visits and Indian engagements indicates that its diplomatic course and policy are shifting towards Nepal. A review of ongoing engagements of Nepal's friends to Nepal's development and their assistance and aid reflect that China-Nepal-India trilateral relations are becoming more viable than before.

Further, when the political parties and their ideology are considered, Nepal's and India's governments have different political ideology but Nepal and China have communist governments. A basic assumption is that Nepal faces challenges in maintaining balanced relations with both neighbours. The perception is that, due to its communist government, some scholars and others predict that Nepal will incline more toward China, which India would perceive as a security threat to Indian security interests. However, it is arguable that, whether governments have the same ideology or not, China always supports those who are in government, as well as their decisions, rather than following communist ideology. On the other hand, India's diplomacy is now slightly changed and has a political tone. Moreover, the cultural factors and open borders are strong influences, so that in the future Nepal, India and China relations will be stronger than in the past. However, one cannot ignore that China and India both have an interest in Nepal and that both nations want to make their presence felt in Nepal.

For Nepal, India has been the key development partner. India had been supporting Nepal in developing projects and political affairs during the insurgency and time of mass movements. India has been assisting Nepal in different sectors through economic assistance to Nepal, such as infrastructure development, capacity development of human resources and initiation of large and intermediate project that have been undertaken with Indian economic assistance. Nepal does not have direct contact to seaports, so its trade depends mostly on the Indian market. India and Nepal have a bilateral treaty on transit, a treaty on trade and agreements of cooperation to control unauthorized trade. The foregoing provides both national investment and trade facilities and provide Nepal with transit facilities to support third country trade.

For China and Nepal, due to geographical structure and complication, there are not many options or routes for trade and transit points between Nepal and China. Only the Rasuwagadhi-Kerung border trade and transit point has been updated to international standards after the great earthquake which damaged the transit point and closed border link roads.

Since the earthquake and the blockade along the Nepal-India border in September 2015, Nepal has become closer to China as it has tried to find alternatives to trade and transit to India, allowing China to step into the Nepali market that was, in past, India's monopoly. Further, according to the diplomat newspaper through the 'One Belt, One Road' initiative, Beijing is looking into the possibility of connecting Kathmandu to Lhasa in Tibet via railways at an estimated cost of $8 billion. China's activities have been steadily expanding in Nepal after Kathmandu's support for OBOR materialized. This happened despite India's stiff resistance to 'OBOR'. So, for both neighbours, Nepal is an important friend for not only their economic interests but also in multilateral and regional fora.

China's engagement in South Asia and Nepal contributes to more assertive diplomacy and friendship between Nepal and India. Meanwhile, both neighbours and Nepal's political parties are reluctant to act based on their ideology but Nepal's government aims for a balanced foreign policy towards its neighbours. According to the Constitution of Nepal, foreign policy of Nepal is guided by abiding faith in the United Nations and the policy of non-alignment. It includes:

- Mutual respect for each other's territorial integrity and sovereignty.
- Non-interference in each other's internal affairs.
- Respect for mutual equality.
- Non-aggression and the peaceful settlement of disputes.
- Cooperation for mutual benefit.

Contact between the people of China and Nepal is restricted. Both countries require visa, unlike with India and Nepal. However, the relations of Nepal and India are cordial, with bilateral agreements. Considering the social and cultural bonds that both countries have in common, it can be said that they are like family. Both countries have people-to-people relations that are stronger than state level, such that the countries are culturally and socially connected.

CHINESE ACTIVISM IN SOUTH ASIA AND TRADITIONAL US INFLUENCE

In the twenty-first century, South Asia has experienced many changes caused by internal and external factors that affected the political stability of South Asian region. Since the 9/11 terrorist attacks, world politics and country polarization have occurred globally, impacting South Asia. This divided nations into two sides concerning the global war against terrorism. US had influence around the world, making India and US a strategic partnership against terrorism and in global issues, which further made India an emerging US ally in South Asian region. In the international forum and among South Asian national issues, the US has tried to view Nepal and other South Asian countries through the Indian perspective, depending on Indian analysis. This strengthened Indian and US influence on South Asian issues in politics, human rights and international cooperation.

Recently, however, the change in leadership in the US and India has had direct effects on the politics and regional alliances and structures. For the structure of power balance in contemporary Asia, India, China, the US and Japan all play vital roles for stability and peace in this region. Leadership that is transformational, reformative and constructive is needed, however, US President Trump's bilateralism policy has already distanced the US. from global and multilateral alliances, which can jeopardy the US global superpower image. This already shows effects on trade, immigration and political fora. In international relations, the US is losing its hegemony. This distancing from the global alliances, resulting from the rejection of the Trans-Pacific Partnership (TPP), the pull-out from the Paris Climate Accords, Jagannathan (2017) places the US at odds with the G7 on an agreement which 195 nations have signed and 147 have formally ratified. This set back the US global superpower image and hegemony in international relations. In the case of South Asian countries, the US had previously expressed their political interest through their alliances, such as with Japan and India, in terms of economics assistance and support and cooperation in global fora.

In contrast to the actions of the US, China is expanding its presence in South Asia and in international relations. In South Asia, China is developing good relations with countries, such as Sri Lanka, Pakistan and Maldives and offering economic assistance without any conditions. As a result, countries that traditionally relied on Indian and US assistance are now accepting Chinese support. Thus, China's trade and growing engagement on this region is bringing other South Asian states under China's influence. China's engagement in Pakistan, for example, with investment in infrastructure projects and collaborations on security and defence, indicate its growing presence in this region.

In the context of possible policy options for Nepal in response to both growing Chinese and US influence and the future consequences of Trump's policy of bilateralism, Nepal can gain advantages from both India and China. Under Trump's policies, Nepal might not continue to get assistance that the US had previously given and as a result suffers. Although Nepal can propose, on its own, conditions in international fora to support US policy which benefit Nepal. However, the current situation is that the US and India are trying to influence Nepal's close relationship and policies towards China, considering these as threats for their superpower image in areas such as refugee issues and human rights issues.

In the context of India and China, there is a significant possibility that both nations will be inclined to support the development of Nepali projects. This inclination is driven by their competitive efforts to establish Nepal as a strategic ally.

CONCLUSION

After the World War Two, the US highlighted its national interest and that became a globalized priority through an emerging new world order. This US policy focused on developing an international order based on economic interdependence and multilateralism and strategic alliances under US leadership. This promoted US leadership and hegemony. Recent changes in leadership and bilateralism show the US distancing itself from global fora. This may cause instability, risk the security of its allies and have a negative impact on globalization. Although, for some, this gives a positive interpretation to the 'America First' slogan, it positions nationalism first, whereas, in this century, almost all elements are interconnected and globalized, requiring multilateralism.

In the larger Asia, South Asia is important, with China, India and Pakistan all nuclear countries. China's activism in South Asia gives it an opportunity to lead the world in terms of trade with India and South Asian states, which gives control of a large market. China's trade with the US and the African continent and its participation in international fora, give China increased influence, particularly considering the US pulling out of international collaborations and commitments.

India and China can contribute in a major way to the stability and development of the South Asian region. In the long term, US traditional relations and influence on security, as well as the US Indian strategic partnership, are still viable, due to Pakistani and Chinese factors. The US India strategic relationship plays a critical role to check the balance between India, China and Pakistan.

Nepal-India relations, relative to increased Chinese influence, provide the possibility of more options for Nepal and India in economic cooperation, with both countries benefiting.

REFERENCES

Chollet, Derek and James Goldgeier, 2008, 'America between the Wars, from 11/9 to 9/11: The Misunderstood Years between the Fall of the Berlin Wall and the Start of the War on Terror'. New York: Public Affairs.

Cronin, Richard, 2005,'The North Korea Nuclear Threat and the U.S. Japan Security Alliance: Perceived Interests, Approaches, and Prospects', *The Fletcher Forum of World Affairs*, vol. 29, no. 1, p. 51-73.

Jagannathan, Meera, 2017, 'Here are all the terrible things President Trump has said about NAFTA—before deciding to stick with it', *New York Daily News*, 27 April 2017, http://www.nydailynews.com/news/politics/terriblepresident-trump-nafta-article-1.3107104 (accessed on 16 June 2018).

Kausikan, Bilahari, 2017, 'Asia in the Trump Era, in Council on Foreign Relations.' https://www.foreignaffairs.com/reviews/review-essay/2017-04-17/asia-trump-era (accessed on 18 March 2018).

Ministry of Foreign Affairs, Nepal, 2018, Nepal India-relation, https://mofa.gov.np/nepal-india-relations/ (accessed on 20 July 2018).

Pant, Harsh V., 2017, 'China's Moment in Nepal: Implications for India' in *The Diplomat*, 27 December 2017. https://thediplomat.com/2017/12/chinas-moment-in-nepal-implications-for-india/ (accessed on 23 July 2018).

Santoro, D. and J. Warden, 2015, 'Assuring Japan and South Korea in the Second Nuclear Age', The Washington Quarterly, 38: 1. <https://twq.elliott.gwu.edu/sites/twq.elliott.gwu.edu/files/downloads/TWQ_Spring2015_Santoro-Warden.pdf> (accessed on 16 June 2018).

Singh, Santosh, 2016, *US Policy and Approach Towards Bangladesh, Nepal and Sri Lanka 1992-2003*, Morrisville: Lulu Publication.

Sutter, Robert G. 2015, 'The United States and Asia: Regional Dynamics and Twenty-First Century Relations', MD, Rowman & Littlefield.

Thapa, Gaurab S., 2018, 'New Outlook in Nepal's Relations with India and China.' In *Asia Times* on 7 May 2018. http://www.atimes.com/new-outlook-in-nepals-relations-with-india-and-china/ (accessed on 25 June 2018).

The Asia Foundation, 2016, 'Asian Views on America's Role in Asia: The Future of the Rebalance: Strategic Recommendations for the Incoming U.S. President on Foreign Policy towards Asia', The vAsia Foundation.

Contributors

BHIM NATH REGMI Associate Professor, Tribhuvan University, Nepal.

NARAYANI DEVKOTA is a lecturer in sociology at Saraswati Multiple Campus, affiliated with Tribhuvan University and regularly contributes articles on contemporary issues to Kantipur National Daily.

PURNA BAHADUR KARKI Ph.D. is a Postdoctoral research fellow at the Institute of Global Studies, Tokyo University of Foreign Studies. Currently, he is engaged in research on Post-Conflict Reconciliations and Challenges in Nepal.

PRABHAT CHHETRI holds an LL.M. in Constitutional Law and International Law from Tribhuvan University. She serves as Assistant Government Attorney at the Office of the Attorney General in Nepal.

REWATI RAJ TRIPATHI Ph.D. Scholar at the Law Campus ofTribhuvan University Exhibition Road, Kathmandu, Nepal. He has previously held a Joint Secretary within the Government of Nepal.

SARMILA BAGALE, Tribhuvan University, Nepal.

SARITA NANDMEHAR, Ph.D. scholar at the Centre for South Asian Studies in Jawaharlal Nehru University (JNU), New Delhi, India.

SHOVA PATHAK is Under Secretary, Government of Nepal. M.A. English (Tribhuvan University), LL.M. Criminal Justice (Purbanchal University).

SHIVA PRASAD PAUDEL (Dr). has earned a Ph.D. in law and a teaching faculty at Kathmandu University School of Law.

SUJIT KUMAR DATTA Professor, at the Department of International Relations, Chittagong University, Chittagong, Bangladesh. He was a doctoral fellow at the School of Political Science and Public Administration, Shandong University, China.

TUMPA PAUL is a doctoral fellow at the School of Political Science and Public Administration, Shandong University, China.

Index